MW00422891

Originally published as *American Airpower Biography: A Survey of the Field*
First edition 1995
Revised edition 1997

**Library of Congress Cataloging-in-Publication Data**

Meilinger, Phillip S., 1948-
   [American airpower biography]
   Airmen and air theory : a review of the sources / Phillip S. Meilinger.
      p. cm.
Rev. ed. of: American airpower biography : a survey of the field, Rev. ed. 1997; also includes The historiography of airpower theory and doctrine, originally published in the Journal of military history, April 2000.
Includes bibliographical references and index.

  1. Aeronautics, Military—United States—Biography. 2. United States. Air Force—Officers—Bibliography. 3. Generals—United States—Biography. 4. Air power—United States—Historiography. I. Meilinger, Phillip S., 1948- Historiography of airpower theory and doctrine. II. Title.

Air University Press
131 West Shumacher Avenue
Maxwell AFB AL 36112-6615

**Disclaimer**

Opinions, conclusions, and recommendations expressed or implied within are solely those of the author and do not necessarily represent the views of Air University, the United States Air Force, the Department of Defense, or any other US government agency. Cleared for public release: distribution unlimited.

# Contents

## PART 1
## Biographies and Autobiographies

**PART 2**

**The Historiography of Airpower
Theory and Doctrine**

# *About the Author*

Col Phillip S. Meilinger

A 1970 graduate of the United States Air Force Academy, Col Phillip S. Meilinger, USAF, retired, received an MA from the University of Colorado and a PhD from the University of Michigan. After a tour at the Academy, Colonel Meilinger was assigned to the Air Staff's doctrine division in the Pentagon, where he wrote and edited numerous Air Force and joint-doctrine publications, worked roles-and-missions issues, and participated in the planning cell for Instant Thunder during the Gulf War of 1991. A command pilot who flew C-130s and HC-130s in both Europe and the Pacific, he has also worked as an operations officer in the Pacific Airlift Control Center at Clark Air Base, Philippines. From 1992 to 1996, Colonel Meilinger served as dean of the School of Advanced Airpower Studies (SAAS), the Air Force's only graduate school for airpower strategists. After leaving SAAS, he served as a professor of strategy at the Naval War College.

His publications include *Hoyt S. Vandenberg: The Life of a General* (1989; reprint, Air Force History and Museums Program, 2000); *10 Propositions Regarding Air Power* (Washington, D.C.: Air Force History and Museums Program, 1995); and several dozen articles and reviews on airpower history and theory in journals such as *Foreign Policy, Armed Forces and Society, Armed Forces Journal International, Comparative Strategy, Journal of Military History,* and *Aerospace Power Journal.* He also edited and contributed to *The Paths of*

*Heaven: The Evolution of Airpower Theory* (Maxwell Air Force Base, Ala.: Air University Press, 1997).

After he retired, Colonel Meilinger became the deputy director of the AEROSPACENTER for Science Applications International Corporation in McLean, Virginia, where he may be reached by E-mail at meilingerp@saic.com.

# Preface

Any researcher knows that a good bibliography, especially an annotated one, is worth its weight in gold. We are all too busy to slog through the mass of information, good and bad, available on any given subject. We hope to separate the wheat from the chaff without actually having to go through the onerous threshing process ourselves. So we talk to experts in the particular area and ask for guidance. Alternatively, we trudge over to the library and ask someone at the reference desk for help. In either case, we usually resort to a specialized bibliography on the topic of interest. That gets us started. My intent in this book is to spin some gold, or at least some silver or bronze, to help overloaded researchers get started in their quest for good sources on airpower.

I wrote the two parts of this book separately and for different audiences. Part one, "Biographies and Autobiographies," appeared as *American Airpower Biography: A Survey of the Field,* published in 1995 by Air University Press, which also issued a revised edition in 1997. I wrote part two, "The Historiography of Airpower Theory and Doctrine," at the request of the editorial board of *The Journal of Military History* after it decided to publish a historiographical article in each quarterly issue. My article on airpower historiography appeared in the April 2000 issue of *JMH.*

I have edited and updated both pieces for this book. I can only hope that my efforts prove useful to long-suffering researchers.

PHILLIP S. MEILINGER
Potomac Falls, Virginia

# PART 1

## Biographies and Autobiographies

# Chapter 1

# **Introduction**

The involvement of people has given history its enduring fascination and popularity. One field within history, biography, has always held special appeal. All of us have a deep interest in knowing how others, perhaps like ourselves, have met challenges, dealt with failure, and accommodated themselves to victory and fame. On a more mundane level, we like to know how great people lived their day-to-day lives and how they handled their loves, shortcomings, attributes, frailties, and quirks. We find comfort in knowing that great men and women were quite human. This knowledge also provides hope and encouragement because it means that even the humblest of us can aspire to greatness.

Certainly, geniuses live among us, but the lives of most of the ones we consider noteworthy are marked by an unexceptional background and a fortuitous turn of events. Sincere, hardworking, and courageous people find themselves in positions of responsibility when circumstances of great pith and moment are thrust upon them. Predicting how individuals will react in such circumstances is remarkably difficult. Often, people groomed for leadership are found wanting in times of crisis, and those who do step forward come from unexpected quarters. Such has been the case with many of our country's great airmen.

This part of the book reviews the state of American airpower biography and autobiography. I have set certain parameters to define the boundaries of my discussion. I discuss biographies and autobiographies, anthologies, and oral histories of military officers who served in senior positions. Thus, although the stories of great aviators like Eddie Rickenbacker, Charles Lindbergh, and Chuck Yeager are important, those men did not command large forces either in combat or in peace; they had only a temporary effect on the development of strategy and doctrine. Similarly excluded are civilian political leaders and industrialists like Stuart Symington and Donald Douglas, even though they played key roles in their own spheres. What follows are the stories—some published, some not—of America's greatest military airmen—some told by themselves, others by biographers. The order of presentation is roughly chronological, according to the time during which these men served. The fact that a surprising number of air luminaries do not appear here means that much work remains to be done.

Chapter 2

# The Airmen

Unfortunately, one of the greater gaps in the historiography of airpower lies in the area of biography. Both Noel Parrish and David MacIsaac in their Harmon Memorial Lectures in Military History commented on this deficiency and encouraged historians to rectify it. Some listened, but too few. At the same time, the dearth of autobiographies by senior airmen is an even greater problem. Surprisingly and significantly, air leaders have published only two memoirs since Curtis LeMay's effort three decades ago. The absence of such personal reminiscences is perhaps even more serious than the lack of biography.

**Mason M. Patrick** was the first real head of American aviation. Although he served as an Army engineer for 30 years, in 1918 Gen John J. Pershing, Patrick's West Point classmate, appointed him commander of the Air Service in France. In Pershing's words, the air arm had many fine people, but they were "running around in circles"; he wanted Patrick to make them go straight. Although he knew virtually nothing about aviation at that point, Patrick was an excellent organizer and administrator. By the end of the war, the Air Service had become an efficient and well-run combat arm. After the armistice, Patrick returned to the Corps of Engineers, but in late 1921 the Air Service recalled him. His predecessor, Charles Menoher, could not get along with the most famous airman of the day, William "Billy" Mitchell, and Menoher lost the resulting power struggle. Because Patrick had managed the difficult airman during the war, he was given the opportunity to do so again. For the next six years, Patrick remained at the helm although Mitchell left the service in 1926. Patrick's memoir *The United States in the Air* (Garden City, N.Y.: Doubleday, Doran, and Co., 1928), as the title implies, is a rather sweeping look at the function and organization of airpower in this country rather than a strictly autobiographical work. A disappointing book written in a leaden style, it provides very few insights into the personalities and issues so turbulent at the time. Except for the oft-repeated story of how Patrick—upon his assumption of command in October 1921—confronted Mitchell and won, it barely mentions the controversial airman. Similarly, the key issues of air strategy during and after the war, the organization of the new air arm and its role in national defense, and its relationships with the Navy are extremely muted. In short, although Patrick was a key player at a most important time in American airpower history, this book sheds little light on anything of importance during that era.

We have two biographies of Patrick. Bruce A. Bingle's "Building the Foundation: Major General Mason Patrick and the Army Air Arm, 1921–1927" (MA thesis, Ohio State University, 1981) does a workmanlike job of presenting a bureaucratic history of the Air Service as seen through Patrick's eyes. A fairly sympathetic account, it portrays the air chief as an airpower advocate as determined as Billy Mitchell but possessing far more tact and political acumen. Missing, however, is more personal insight into Patrick's personality and leadership style.

A far more important effort is Robert White's *Mason Patrick and the Fight for Air Service Independence* (Washington, D.C.: Smithsonian Institution Press, forthcoming). White argues convincingly that Patrick was the real impetus behind reforms in the Army's air arm after World War I; specifically, he was largely responsible for passage of the landmark Air Corps Act of 1926. Although the flamboyant Mitchell often overshadowed Patrick, White argues that Patrick's low-key style, extensive and friendly contacts within the Army hierarchy, and quiet but relentless pressure achieved results, whereas more aggressive actions would have failed. He also shows that Patrick began as a skeptic, but over his years as Air Service chief, his strategic vision broadened, and he became a staunch advocate of airpower. By the mid-1920s, he had become a believer in both "independent air operations" and the growing dominance of airpower in war. Unlike Mitchell, however, Patrick believed that it would take a long time to establish an independent air force. The Air Corps Act was a transitional but necessary step towards that goal—nothing more radical could have gotten through Congress.

More significantly, because of his long background as an engineer, Patrick was well aware of the need for a sound logistics base and industrial infrastructure to back airpower. In his view, without the existence of a robust aeronautical industry in the United States that included a powerful commercial-aviation component, the Air Service would remain merely a collection of airplanes. Towards that end, Patrick totally revamped the Air Service engineering division at Wright Field, Ohio, taking it out of the aircraft-design business—which had produced a series of costly failures—and made it responsible for testing the designs provided by commercial builders.

White's handling of Patrick's relationship with Mitchell is balanced and believable. Patrick realized that Mitchell was a highly talented and innovative leader who inspired his men to great efforts, but he also understood that Mitchell needed firm supervision to prevent self-inflicted wounds. Significantly, virtually all of the hot water in which Mitchell found himself throughout his career occurred either before Patrick's tenure as Air Service chief or after Mitchell left his guidance.

Patrick left behind few papers, so White's book contains regrettably few details about either his personal life or his 40-year Army career before his duty with the Air Service. Overall, however, it is an excellent effort.

**William "Billy" Mitchell** is the most famous and controversial figure in the history of American airpower. The son of a wealthy Wisconsin senator, he enlisted as a private during the Spanish-American War. Quickly gaining a commission due to the intervention of his father, he joined the Signal Corps. He became an outstanding junior officer, displaying a rare degree of initiative, courage, and leadership. After challenging tours in the Philippines and Alaska, Mitchell was assigned to the General Staff—at the time its youngest member. He slowly became excited about aviation—then part of the Signal Corps—and in 1916 at age 38, he took private flying lessons.

Arriving in France in April 1917, only a few days after the United States had entered the war, Lieutenant Colonel Mitchell met extensively with British and French air leaders and studied their operations. Quickly taking charge, he began preparations for the American air units that would follow. The story of the mobilization of American aviation in World War I is not a glorious one. Months passed before pilots arrived in France and even more before aircraft arrived. Nevertheless, Mitchell rapidly earned a reputation as a daring, flamboyant, and tireless leader. He eventually became a brigadier general and commanded all American combat units in France. In September 1918, he planned and led nearly 1,500 Allied aircraft in the air phase of the Saint-Mihiel offensive. Recognized as the top American combat airman of the war (he received the Distinguished Service Cross, the Distinguished Service Medal, and several foreign decorations), Mitchell still managed to alienate most of his superiors—both flying and nonflying—during his 18 months in France.

Returning to the United States in early 1919, Mitchell became deputy chief of the Air Service, retaining his one-star rank. His relations with superiors continued to sour as he began to attack both the War and Navy Departments for their lack of foresight regarding airpower. His fight with the Navy climaxed with the dramatic bombing tests of 1921 and 1923 that sank several battleships, proving—at least to Mitchell—the obsolescence of surface fleets. Within the Army, he also experienced difficulties, notably with his superiors Charles Menoher and, later, Mason Patrick. In early 1925, he reverted to his permanent rank of colonel and was transferred to Texas. Although such demotions were not unusual at the time—Major General Patrick himself had reverted to colonel upon returning to the Corps of Engineers in 1919—many people interpreted the move as punishment and exile. Not content to remain quiet, when the Navy dirigible *Shenandoah* crashed in a storm, killing 14 of the crew, Mitchell issued his famous statement accusing senior leaders in the Army and Navy of incompetence and "almost treasonable administration of the national defense." He was court-martialed, found guilty of insubordination, and suspended from active duty for five years without pay. Instead, Mitchell elected to resign as of 1 February 1926 and spent the next decade writing and preaching the gospel of airpower to all who would listen. Mitchell viewed the election of Franklin D. Roosevelt as advantageous for airpower even though Roosevelt was a Navy man. In fact, he believed that the new president would appoint him assistant secretary of war for air or perhaps even secretary of defense in a new and unified military organization. Such hopes never materialized. Mitchell died in 1936 of a variety of ailments, including a bad heart and influenza.

Unquestionably, the most balanced and useful treatment of this important airman is Alfred F. Hurley's *Billy Mitchell, Crusader for Air Power*, rev. ed. (Bloomington, Ind.: Indiana University Press, 1975). Hurley deals sparingly with the general's early career and personal life, concentrating instead on his war experiences, the postwar years, and his theories of airpower employment. Mitchell was the first prominent American to espouse publicly a vision of strategic airpower that would dominate future war. He believed that aircraft were inherently offensive, strategic weapons that revolutionized war by allowing a direct attack on an enemy country's "vital centers"—the mighty industrial areas that produced the vast amount of armaments and equipment so necessary in modern war. He did not consider such use of aircraft either illegal or immoral. In fact, in light of the trench carnage of World War I that slaughtered millions, he argued that airpower provided a quicker and more humane method of waging war. To carry out this mission of strategic attack effectively, he argued for the necessity of separating aviation from the traditional, surface-oriented Army and Navy. Mitchell's persistent gibes at the Navy were especially nasty, and Hurley argues that they not only fostered bitter interservice rivalry but also spurred the Navy to greater efforts in developing carrier-based aviation—precisely the opposite of Mitchell's intent. Nevertheless, Hurley concludes that these shortcomings were more than offset by Mitchell's vision

9

and foresight regarding the future of war, later proved sub-stantially correct, which sustained the fledgling Air Force dur-ing its early, difficult years.

Most of the other published accounts of Mitchell's life are hagiographies written during or soon after World War II that depict him as a prophet without honor and as a martyr for air-power. Surprisingly, few of them discuss his airpower theories, concentrating instead on the sensational aspects of his career. The best of this genre is Isaac Don Levine's *Mitchell, Pioneer of Air Power,* rev. ed. (New York: Duell, Sloan and Pearce, 1958). Levine addresses Mitchell's personal life, including his early years as a junior officer, basing his story largely on letters and interviews. Although he includes no notes or bibliography, Levine obviously did a great deal of research. Unfortunately, besides employing overly breathless prose, the book glorifies Mitchell and ignores his very real character flaws. Mitchell was vain, petulant, racist, overbearing, and egotistical. Although his aggressive advocacy of airpower proved entertaining and won much publicity, his antics probably had little effect on swaying either public opinion or Congress. Indeed, one could even argue that his incessant and vicious attacks on the Navy did more harm than good and induced an animosity between sailors and airmen that has never really abated.

Biographies that have, frankly, little value include Emile Gauvreau and Lester Cohen's *Billy Mitchell, Founder of Our Air Force and Prophet without Honor* (New York: E. P. Dutton and Co., Inc., 1942); Roger Burlingame's *General Billy Mitchell, Champion of Air Defense* (New York: McGraw-Hill, 1952); and Ruth Mitchell's *My Brother Bill, The Life of General "Billy" Mitchell* (New York: Harcourt, Brace, 1953). His sister's book does, however, quote heavily from Mitchell's unpublished manuscript describing his tour in Alaska from 1901 to 1903. This little-known story of the Signal Corps's efforts to string a telegraph line across the territory is quite interesting. Burke Davis's *The Billy Mitchell Affair* (New York: Random House, 1967), a cut above those just mentioned, is unique in that it covers in some detail Mitchell's famous report of his visit to Hawaii in 1924. In that document, he predicted a future war with Japan that opened with a carrier-based air attack on

Pearl Harbor. Additionally, Davis, who had access to the transcript of Mitchell's court-martial, covers that event fairly extensively. Although his treatment is evenhanded, it tends to put the airman in a favorable light, portraying him as a victim of Army conservatism.

Michael L. Grumelli's "Trial of Faith: The Dissent and Court-Martial of Billy Mitchell" (PhD diss., Rutgers University, 1991) takes a different view of the court proceedings. This absorbing and detailed account of Mitchell's 1925 trial for insubordination argues that the general was convicted not only because he was guilty as charged but also because his defense lawyer, who bungled cross-examinations, proved woefully inept. Furthermore, a clever prosecutor produced testimony from expert witnesses revealing that virtually all of Mitchell's charges of military incompetence and negligence were unfounded. Grumelli concludes that Mitchell's decision to provoke a public court-martial was a serious miscalculation that quickly revealed his "tremendous arrogance, extreme self-righteousness, gross exaggerations and blatant inaccuracies." He further concludes that Mitchell, surprised at his conviction, spent the rest of his life vainly seeking vindication but faded quickly into obscurity, devoid of either influence or importance. His rejection by Roosevelt for a senior post in the administration was the last straw.

Raymond R. Flugel's "United States Air Power Doctrine: A Study of the Influence of William Mitchell and Giulio Douhet at the Air Corps Tactical School, 1921–1935" (PhD diss., University of Oklahoma, 1965) argues that a direct link existed between the two air theorists. Flugel even argues that Mitchell's writings owed a heavy but unacknowledged debt to Douhet, basing this charge on the discovery of a partial translation of Douhet's *Command of the Air* dated 1922 (published in Italian in 1921) in the Air Service archives. This predates by a decade a French edition translated for the Air Corps by Dorothy Benedict and George Kenney. Unfortunately, this discovery—an important one indeed—is totally wasted by the author's flawed methodology. Through textual analysis of *Command of the Air,* Flugel attempts to show that Mitchell's writings of the mid-1920s and the Air Corps Tactical School (ACTS) textbooks of the same era plagiarized Douhet. He actually reproduces several paragraphs, underlining words and phrases to show their similarity. However, rather than using the newly discovered 1922 translation that he trumpets—presumably available to Mitchell—Flugel relies instead on the Dino Ferrari translation of 1942! Because the two versions have significant differences, Flugel's charges remain unproven.

Published over two decades after his death, Mitchell's *Memoirs of World War I: From Start to Finish of Our Greatest War* (New York: Random House, 1960) compiles his experiences in France from April 1917 to the armistice, based on his diaries (now lost, parts of which appeared serially in *Liberty* magazine in 1928). As with any such work, no one can tell how many of its opinions and predictions were of later device. Not surprisingly, Mitchell comes across looking quite prescient concerning the unfolding of the war. The book does, however, reveal some notable matters. It makes apparent, for example, Mitchell's distaste and low regard for Benjamin Foulois, his nominal superior. It is a pity that two of the most senior and important American airmen, who should have been close allies in their advocacy of airpower, were bitter enemies. Also apparent is Mitchell's remarkable curiosity about all things regarding air warfare. *Memoirs of World War I* is replete with descriptions of myriad and diverse details, such as what time weather reports arrived at a fighter squadron and in what format, the construction of shock absorbers on a captured German aircraft, and the type of parachutes used by balloon observers. One other revealing aspect of this memoir is Mitchell's already emerging disdain for "nonflying officers" in Washington who "know nothing about airpower" yet try to direct its course. According to this book, Mitchell returned to the United States in 1919 already convinced of the need for a separate service liberated from the control of narrow-minded surface officers.

Another notable work of Mitchell's is *General Greely: The Story of a Great American* (New York: G. P. Putnam's, 1936). Adolphus W. Greely, one of the more interesting characters of his era, fought in the Civil War, strung telegraph wire across the southwest United States, and made a name for himself internationally as an Arctic explorer. In 1887 he received a promotion to brigadier general and became chief signal officer of the US Army, a post he held until his retirement in 1906. During those two decades, he modernized the Signal Corps dramatically, but, perhaps most significantly, he pushed for a rejuvenation of the Balloon Corps and encouraged experimentation in heavier-than-air flight. Although Greely retired before the Wright brothers sold their first airplane to the Army's Signal Corps, Mitchell credits him with creating an atmosphere of innovation that made such a contract possible. Mitchell's use of this biography as a vehicle for recounting some of his own experiences as a junior officer in Greely's Signal Corps gives us some insights into his activities during the Spanish-American War, his tour in the Philippines during the insurrection there, and his rugged adventures in Alaska. Mitchell wrote this biography in 1935, the year Greely died; it came out in print the following year, soon after Mitchell's own death.

**Benjamin D. Foulois** taught himself to fly, largely through correspondence with the Wright brothers in 1909. Although many of his contemporaries died in plane crashes or quit flying, he continued as an operational pilot until World War I. He then went to France, where, as a brigadier general, he had responsibility for all Air Service support functions. After the war, he served as an air attaché in Germany, commanded Mitchel Field in New York, and in 1931 became chief of the Air Corps.

John F. Shiner's *Foulois and the U.S. Army Air Corps, 1931–1935* (Washington, D.C.: Office of Air Force History, 1984) is a solid treatment of the Air Corps chief and his times. Foulois came from a humble background and was physically unimpressive; worse, he lacked the charisma of his contemporary and chief rival within the air arm, Billy Mitchell. Nevertheless, Shiner argues that Foulois's steady perseverance in working to shift War Department views regarding the importance of airpower gradually paid off, resulting in the increased autonomy of the General Headquarters (GHQ) Air Force, formed in 1935. On the other hand, perhaps because of his humble origins, Foulois was not popular among his Army brethren. Moreover, the disastrous performance of the Air Corps in the airmail fiasco of 1934 (probably more Foulois's fault than Shiner acknowledges) earned him the ill will of President Roosevelt. Looking for a scapegoat, Congress—also embarrassed by the miserable Air Corps performance—held hearings on the issue of aircraft procurement. Foulois was reprimanded for "misleading" Congress and violating the spirit of procurement laws. The Air Corps chief's relations with the Navy were also stormy during this period. But in truth, given the budget crunch during the bottom of the Great Depression, their inherently conflicting views regarding the role of airpower in war, and the poisoned atmosphere created by Mitchell, such difficulties were inevitable. Without friends in or out of the Army and with his usefulness clearly limited, Foulois retired in December 1935, a bitter and lonely man.

Shiner depicts Foulois as a poor administrator, noting that he was not a deep thinker and did little to foster the development of strategic-airpower doctrine during his tenure. Nevertheless, this was the golden age for such development in the Air Corps, and Shiner credits Foulois with creating a climate that allowed such intellectual ferment to occur. Overall, his book is a solid account of an important figure.

With the help of C. V. Glines, Foulois tells his story in *From the Wright Brothers to the Astronauts: The Memoirs of Benjamin D. Foulois* (New York: McGraw-Hill, 1968), an exciting, witty, and enjoyable memoir that combines insightful details about the early years of American aviation and an explanation of Foulois's own conduct during World War I and his years as Air Corps chief. The most illuminating aspect of this book, however, is the gusto with which Foulois attacks Billy Mitchell. Foulois reveals that the animosity between him and Mitchell began in 1916, when Foulois accompanied the 1st Aero Squadron to Mexico with Pershing in a futile attempt to catch the bandit Pancho Villa. At the same time, the chief of the Signal Corps had to leave office due to financial improprieties, and Mitchell, who had not yet even flown an airplane, became temporary chief. The poor performance of the aviation unit in Mexico resulted in mutual finger pointing between Mitchell and Foulois, and the rift never healed. Mitchell's World War I memoirs—not published until 1960—apparently offended Foulois (Mitchell refers to him as an incompetent "carpetbagger" who "no longer flew"). So Foulois decided to tell his side of the story at age 86 and "set the record straight." He portrays Mitchell as an inept braggart who was all talk and no action, a lousy pilot, and a prima donna who did more harm than good. The truth, as usual, probably lies between these two extremes. Pershing clearly respected both of them but thought that neither had the experience or maturity to run the Air Service; hence, he appointed Mason Patrick to lead the air arm and control its two main recalcitrants. Overall, Foulois delivers good pyrotechnics and an entertaining read.

**Oscar M. Westover** succeeded Foulois as chief of the Air Corps, holding that position from 1935 to 1938. Originally, Westover was a balloonist, and fellow airmen saw him as insufficiently air-minded. Precisely for that reason, he was popular with the General Staff, who thus named him Foulois's successor. He died in a plane crash in September 1938, and Henry H. "Hap" Arnold became chief. It is interesting to speculate whether he would have played a role in the expansion of the Air Corps in the years leading up to Pearl Harbor or if, like Malin Craig in the Army, he would have been shunted aside just as the crisis approached. No one has written a biography of Westover, but Frank Faulkner includes a chapter on him in his handbook *Westover: Man, Base and Mission* (Springfield, Mass.: Hungry Hill Press, 1990). Decidedly not analytical, this chapter is little more than an expanded resume that lists his various assignments and promotion dates; however, it does contain a number of interesting photographs.

Air Force historian James L. Crowder Jr.'s discovery of a footlocker containing the personal papers of Maj Gen **Clarence L. Tinker** led him to write a biography of this unusual airman—an Osage Indian and the first American general officer to die in World War II (Tinker's B-17 went down at the Battle of Midway in June 1942). In *Osage General: Maj. Gen. Clarence L. Tinker* (Tinker AFB, Okla.: Office of History, Oklahoma City Air Logistics Center, 1987), Crowder states that his book "is neither a psychological analysis of the individual nor a study of aviation doctrine in the emerging air force." Rather, it is a mildly interesting, if somewhat chatty, account of Tinker's military career and life.

Although the book tells us nothing of Tinker's theory of air warfare, his speeches during the war reflect his strong advocacy of strategic airpower. *Osage General's* major flaw is that, instead of relating what made Tinker successful, it dwells upon his personal life and character traits. Although one might find such information useful, the fact that it comes from an adoring wife, sister, and daughter renders it something less than completely reliable. Thus, we find much anecdotal information but little real analysis. Nevertheless, the bulk of the book is a workmanlike story of a career soldier during peacetime who served in many capacities all over the world. A man who loved to fly, Tinker was highly competent, well respected within the Air Corps, and probably destined for high rank and responsibility had he lived.

Photo courtesy of HomeOfHeroes.com

Although not an aviator, **William A. Moffett** was chosen to form the Navy's Bureau of Aeronautics in 1921. He had served over two decades as a surface sailor, won the Medal of Honor for action at Veracruz in 1914, and commanded the battleship *Mississippi* from 1918 to 1920. Despite his lack of experience in aviation, he was one of the first high-ranking naval officers to appreciate the importance of the airplane and the impact it would have on the fleet. He eagerly accepted the challenge of forming an aeronautical bureau within the Navy and proved extremely successful in this endeavor. Because aviation was a politically and militarily contentious issue throughout the interwar period, Moffett had to use all of his diplomacy, tact, tenacity, and savvy to see the infant air arm through its formative years. He did, however, have an unfortunate affection for airships, a technological dead end that squandered millions of dollars. Ironically, in April 1933 he jumped on board the airship *Akron* for a flight from Lakehurst, New Jersey, to Newport, Rhode Island. The ship went down in a severe storm off the coast of New Jersey, killing Moffett and most of the crew.

William F. Trimble writes about the life of this "essential man" in *Admiral William A. Moffett, Architect of Naval Aviation* (Washington, D.C.: Smithsonian Institution Press, 1994), an excellent book that gives a clear and sympathetic portrait of Moffett, arguing that his firm but enlightened leadership proved essential to the successful development of naval aviation. Despite the presence of many younger, more aggressive, and more knowledgeable naval aviators, Moffett's strong background as a surface officer gave him credibility and won his superiors' trust—qualities the others could not match. Moffett did not challenge his superiors, as did Billy Mitchell in the Army, and he did not demand a separate service. Instead, he preached the necessity of keeping aviation an integral part of the fleet. He told his young aviators to always remember that they were naval officers first and airmen second, a deft and crucial handling of the loyalty issue that, Trimble implies, saved the air arm from amputation. At the same time, the author argues that Mitchell's tactics and his propaganda campaign provided Moffett the lever he needed to energize the naval hierarchy to form the aeronautical bureau. In this balanced account, Trimble notes that Moffett, often dictatorial and stubborn, tended to push projects like large airships and small aircraft carriers long after it was clear they were bad ideas. Nevertheless, the admiral was indeed the right man at the right time. Without his vision and political acumen, naval aviation would have evolved far differently.

Photo courtesy of Ralph Cooper

In *Admiral John H. Towers: The Struggle for Naval Air Supremacy* (Annapolis: Naval Institute Press, 1991), Clark G. Reynolds relates the history of American naval aviation from its earliest days to the dawn of the nuclear age, as seen through the eyes of premier naval aviator **John H. Towers**. It recounts the "struggle" of Towers and his fellow airmen not only against the Japanese but also against the Army and nonaviators within their own service.

Reynolds's account of these early years (Towers entered aviation in 1911) is detailed and fascinating. Surprisingly, in these difficult and dangerous times, early naval aviators began resenting and questioning the actions of fellow seamen who did not fly. Depicted as traditional, conservative, and closed to new ideas, surface sailors are charged with deliberately retarding naval aviation by holding up budgets, promotions, and doctrinal reform. Similarly, naval aviators suspected as early as 1914 that Army airmen had designs on their planes, pilots, and missions. Billy Mitchell's attacks on the Navy after 1919 served to confirm these fears.

The bulk of this book deals with Towers's role behind the scenes in Washington and then in Hawaii during World War II. Never holding a combat command, Towers instead played a key role in planning, mobilizing, and administering the Navy at war. Although his is an important story, it is not a dazzling one. Yet, Towers was important as one of the first and most innovative tactical thinkers regarding carrier operations. Early wartime experience proved the accuracy of two of his earliest admonitions—that carriers should be employed in task forces rather than singly or as part of a battleship flotilla and that they should never venture within range of land-based airpower until the establishment of air superiority. Moreover, from his position as chief of the Bureau of Naval Aeronautics in Washington, Towers selected those airmen, his protégés, who would command the carriers in combat. Surprisingly, however, Reynolds's portrait is not complimentary. Towers emerges as vain, ambitious, overbearing, political, and paranoid. Perhaps the most damning depiction of him concerns his vociferous efforts to block unification of the armed forces after the war. Towers played a leading role in the sorry story of the Navy's attempts to prevent the formation of the Defense Department and the Joint Chiefs of Staff (JCS), fearing they would encroach upon Navy prerogatives.

Clark Reynolds is a masterful naval historian; his research is prodigious; and his writing style is pleasant. His book, however, lacks a concluding chapter that sums up Towers the man and his impact on American military affairs. Overall, *Admiral John H. Towers* is an important work about a largely forgotten figure.

**Henry H. "Hap" Arnold** was one of the truly great men in American airpower. Taught to fly at the Wright brothers' flying school in 1911, he rose steadily in rank and responsibility throughout the 1920s and 1930s and became commanding general of the Army Air Forces (AAF) during World War II. In 1944 he was promoted to five-star rank, but his poor health—he suffered several heart attacks during the war—forced him to retire six months after Japan surrendered. Thomas M. Coffey's *Hap: The Story of the U.S. Air Force and the Man Who Built It, General Henry "Hap" Arnold* (New York: Viking Press, 1982), which relies heavily on interviews and memoirs of Arnold's contemporaries to portray his life, is an interesting though incomplete study.

Graduating from West Point in 1907, Arnold had hoped to join the cavalry. However, due to his dismal performance as a cadet, he instead found himself in the infantry. After a tour in the Philippines, he reapplied to the cavalry but was again refused. Largely out of a desire to escape the infantry, Arnold then applied for the Signal Corps and became one of America's first military pilots. Aviation was extremely dangerous in those early days, and after several crashes and near crashes, Arnold grounded himself. After more than three years of desk work, he overcame his fears and returned to flying. Because of his relatively extensive experience in aviation, he was forced to remain in Washington on the Air Service staff during World War I, much to his chagrin. For the following two decades, he commanded wings and bases, became a protégé of Billy Mitchell, twice won the Mackay Trophy for aeronautical achievement, received the Distinguished Flying Cross for leading a flight of B-10 bombers to Alaska to display the range of strategic airpower, and became assistant to the chief of the Air Corps in 1935. When Oscar Westover was killed in a plane crash in 1938, Arnold succeeded him as chief. In this position, he was instrumental in laying the groundwork for the massive industrial expansion the war required. During the war itself, he sat as an equal member of the JCS, responsible for guiding the air strategy of the various theaters. Belying his nickname "Hap" (short for "happy"), Arnold was a difficult taskmaster, continually interfering in the affairs of his subordinates and refusing to use or even organize his staff effectively. His mercurial temper often made him quite nasty. Nevertheless, his great weaknesses were also his great strengths. His drive, vision, and sense of initiative proved indispensable in leading the air arm.

Coffey has done an excellent job of bringing Arnold's complex personality to life. Although his portrait is largely sympathetic, Coffey leaves one with the image of a difficult and irascible husband, father, subordinate, and commander. Yet, Arnold's genius for accomplishing great things and inspiring others to do likewise is apparent. Because the author relies so heavily on interviews, however, his story is incomplete and biased. For example, Arnold's decision to personally command B-29 forces in the Pacific was an unprecedented action for a member of the joint chiefs. Although Coffey notes this, he fails to explain how Arnold was able to convince the other chiefs— to say nothing of the theater commanders involved—to accept such an unusual command arrangement. More significantly, although Coffey alludes to Arnold's vision as an air strategist and strategic-bombing advocate, he gives readers almost no insight into this area and scarcely mentions Arnold's extensive writings on this subject (he authored or coauthored four books plus his memoirs). As a result, this biography is more of a sketch than a portrait, providing an outline and some intriguing hints but lacking detail.

Flint O. DuPre's *Hap Arnold: Architect of American Air Power* (New York: Macmillan, 1972), a fairly short character sketch based on Arnold's memoirs, is of little use. Murray Green, however, spent several years conducting an enormous amount of research on Arnold, including dozens of interviews with friends, family, and colleagues. He began work on a biography, tentatively titled "Hap Arnold and the Birth of the United States Air Force," a draft that takes Arnold up to the start of World War II. Unfortunately, he never completed it. Despite the fact that this draft covers only the first 20 years of Arnold's career, it remains an excellent start. Green's in-depth research offers insights and provides information not available elsewhere: Arnold's cadet experiences and the unique culture of West Point at the turn of the century, his relationship with Charles Lindbergh and the America First organization, and the general's problems with President Roosevelt concerning the shipment of aircraft to Europe in the late 1930s. One can find Green's unfinished manuscript in the Special Collections Branch of the Air Force Academy library, along with all the notes and interviews he conducted over the years.

Dik A. Daso takes an extremely interesting and fresh look at Arnold in *Architects of American Air Supremacy: Gen Hap Arnold and Dr. Theodore von Kármán* (Maxwell AFB, Ala.: Air University Press, 1997). Daso explores one of the general's most unusual facets: his fascination with technology. Airmen have always been known for their affinity for and reliance upon machines, but Arnold had a particularly well honed appreciation for the importance of technology to airpower. Having true airpower and not just a collection of airplanes required that a country possess the industrial infrastructure to design and build aircraft and their engines. For the United States, this meant a powerful aviation industry, airline industry, airway structure, and—most importantly—a research and development (R&D) base second to none. From his earliest years as an officer, Arnold realized these truths, and during his assignment to Washington in World War I, he witnessed firsthand how a lack of these assets could lead to waste and ineffectiveness. For the rest of his career, Arnold strove to ensure that such problems would not recur.

Daso does a masterful job of detailing Arnold's efforts to build a link between the Air Force and the technological base upon which it so heavily depended. His approach is especially useful in that he intertwines Arnold's career with that of his close colleague Dr. Theodore von Kármán, the brilliant, Hungarian-born aeronautical engineer. The climax of Daso's work comes with the discussion of "Toward New Horizons," the futuristic vision statement commissioned by Arnold and produced by Kármán in December 1945. This intellectual tour de force, which foresaw with remarkable clarity the evolution of the Air Force in, inter alia, space, ballistic missiles, unmanned air vehicles, and cruise missiles, served as the blueprint for technological development in the Air Force for the next three decades. Daso's work is an important addition to the literature, not only about Hap Arnold but more generally about the vital interface between technology and airpower. Because the Arnold family granted the author access to a wealth of information previously unavailable to researchers, he was able to shed new light on Arnold's personality.

Daso then wrote another, more complete, biography of Arnold titled *Hap Arnold and the Evolution of American Airpower* (Washington, D.C.: Smithsonian Institution Press, 2000), an excellent effort that covers Arnold's early career and personality in far more detail than we have seen previously. Once again, he focuses on Arnold's zeal in ensuring a close relationship between airpower and technology. Daso also identifies Arnold's holistic approach to airpower as one of his great insights. The United States needed a strong industrial base; a robust R&D program; a broad aviation infrastructure; a large pool of qualified personnel; and, perhaps most importantly, a clearly devised, coherent, and codified doctrine for employing those air assets. Possessing an unshakeable belief in the importance of strategic airpower, Arnold labored to ensure that America possessed all of these necessary elements.

One of the most interesting and insightful portions of this account is the epilogue, wherein Daso expands upon a letter that Arnold wrote shortly before his death regarding his views on leadership. The general noted several vital qualities: technical competence, hard work, vision, judgment, communication skills, a facility for human relations, and integrity. One could also add mental and physical courage. As he progressed in command and responsibility, Arnold continuously faced tough decisions. Having the courage to do the right thing regardless of the consequences and regardless of the effect on friends and family is enormously difficult. This list of attributes, which Arnold displayed in abundance throughout his career, serves as the perfect summation for both the book and the man.

One might quibble with Daso over what his book omits. For example, he spends almost no time discussing broad issues of strategy in World War II, targeting debates, interservice rivalries, or Arnold's relationships with his commanders. Furthermore, it is useful to note here that Arnold was indeed "commanding general" of the AAF, his official title, insofar as he had far more control over his air forces and personnel than does a present-day chief of staff. Had Daso elected to explore this subject, it no doubt would have made for interesting reading.

Nevertheless, Daso's research is prodigious, the numerous illustrations are excellent, and his writing style is eminently pleasing. *Hap Arnold and the Evolution of American Airpower* is an excellent biography of a great commander and is must reading for airmen of all ranks. It is by far the best book written on Arnold to date.

William R. Laidlaw assisted Arnold in writing *Global Mission* (New York: Harper and Row, 1949), memoirs that tend to resemble the man who wrote them: energetic, enthusiastic, advocative, mixing broad vision and intimate detail, and somewhat disorganized. Arnold's legendary temper is not in evidence here. Obviously, he had mellowed in the four years since his retirement; thus, the spirited arguments with the other services—and even with individuals in his own service—

are muted. Arnold notes his differences with the Navy, but he has nary a contrary word for Adm William Leahy, Adm Ernest King, Adm Chester Nimitz, or Adm John Towers, his main antagonists. Although such restraint is commendable, it finesses some of the key strategic issues of the war, and we are left with rather bland comments like, "After some discussion we were able to reach a compromise." He reserves his biggest barbs for the Chinese—whom he saw as hopelessly corrupt—and the Soviets—whom he viewed with increasing distrust as the war progressed. By the end of the war, Arnold was already a cold warrior, and he concluded his memoirs with a warning to maintain an air force powerful enough to counter the Soviet Union. Especially useful are his fascinating stories of the early years of aviation and the evolution of airpower in the two decades following World War I. His detailed account of the war years is also quite insightful, and the sheer number of problems he encountered is clearly illustrated. In seven pages, he lists the subjects of dozens of memos he had to write in a typical day—everything from the design of buttons (actually miniature compasses designed to assist downed aircrews) to the location of B-29 bases in China. Overall, *Global Mission* is an enjoyable and very readable book—one of the best of the wartime memoirs of a senior leader.

The corpus of airpower literature contains very few sound biographies of American airmen involved in engineering or logistical matters. With his biography *Every Inch a Soldier: Augustine Warner Robins and the Building of U.S. Airpower* (College Station, Tex.: Texas A&M University Press, 1995), William Head, an official historian with the Air Force, helps fill this void with a study of perhaps the first and most important of the air logisticians. **Warner Robins** was born in Virginia in 1882 to a patrician family whose men had fought in the Revolutionary War, the War of 1812, and the Civil War. Following in such footsteps, he entered West Point in 1903, the same class as Hap Arnold. After graduating in 1907, Robins spent a decade in the cavalry, and in 1916 his troop accompanied General Pershing to New Mexico for the "punitive expedition" against Pancho Villa. The famous Mexican bandit escaped, but Robins did not. Intrigued by the possibilities of flight embodied in one of the other units on the border—the 1st Aero Squadron, a group of flimsy airplanes engaged in reconnaissance operations—he submitted his papers for a transfer to the air arm.

Because of his relatively senior rank—he was a major by that point—Robins found himself in an administrative position almost as soon as he won his wings. Although he thereby missed the chance to serve in France, Robins did establish a reputation as a first-rate organizer. In 1919 he was assigned to the Supply Division of the Air Service, and, in a sense, he never really left. For the next 20 years, Warner Robins would toil in the world of logistics, mostly at Wright Field in Ohio. These crucial, if not glamorous, assignments put him in the forefront of technological development. Airpower remained only a word unless industry developed and built planes to carry out the theories of the air advocates. Combined with this need, however, was the contradictory requirement to cut spending for defense in a period of fiscal conservatism heightened by the Great Depression—a tremendously challenging situation for an airman in Robins's position.

Head tells us that Robins became an outstanding logistician, largely responsible for putting the Air Service—later the Air Corps—on a sound administrative footing. He instituted a supply-accountability system that remained in effect until the advent of computers 30 years later. Likewise, in 1927 he moved to open a logistics school for nonflying officers to obviate the need to rely upon officers transferred from the cavalry! Missing from this account are details of precisely how Robins went about his task and how his ideas differed from standard practice. Clearly, however, the author's conclusion regarding his subject's impact is accurate—a series of air chiefs found his work indispensable. As the air arm expanded between the wars and as its materiel functions became more complex, Robins advanced in rank to assume greater responsibility for these efforts. In 1935 he was promoted to brigadier general—one of only four in the Air Corps at the time—and assumed command of the Materiel Division at Wright Field.

For the next four years, Robins oversaw the entire logistical side of the Air Corps. He pushed hard for increased funding for R&D, as well as for key technologies ranging from the B-17 to the Norden bombsight to the high-octane gasoline needed to power new, high-performance engines. More importantly, he headed the logistics end of the air arm just as the country began its massive expansion for World War II.

An indifferent pilot, Robins suffered a nearly fatal crash in 1921 that broke his jaw and right arm; the following year, he also developed severe high blood pressure. Each year thereafter, passing his physical became a chore, and in some cases he had to check into a hospital two weeks prior to the exam to bring his condition under sufficient control to get a clean bill of health. In 1939 he took over Air Training Command in Texas, but in June of the following year, the stress of approaching war, combined with his poor health, resulted in a fatal heart attack at the age of 57. Three years later, the Warner Robins Army Air Depot at Robins Field, Georgia, was dedicated to his honor.

Head has written an enjoyable and heavily researched account of an important airman. Not an overly exciting subject, logistics nevertheless remains absolutely essential to military operations. As the old adage goes, "Amateurs discuss strategy, but professionals talk about logistics." Warner Robins played a key role in establishing a foundation for Air Force logistics that would stand the test of war and the transition to an independent service.

Movies and novels have immortalized **Claire L. Chennault,** one of America's more famous airmen and leader of the Flying Tigers. He also has been the subject of a number of biographies—probably more than he deserves. The best of these is certainly Martha Byrd's *Chennault: Giving Wings to the Tiger* (University, Ala.: University of Alabama

Press, 1987), a portrait of someone who at turns could be gruff, stubborn, iconoclastic, gentle, or cultured.

Chennault arrived at ACTS in 1930 with a reputation as a premier pursuit pilot. His ideas concerning pursuit employment evolved from much thought and practical experience. But Air Corps doctrine was shifting decisively in favor of bombardment, and Chennault's attempts to stem that tide proved futile. As Byrd points out, Chennault's abrasive personality negated his arguments, and his colleagues found it more satisfying simply to ignore him. Suffering from a variety of physical ailments and realizing that his theories were out of tune with Air Corps policy, he retired in 1937. Soon after, he moved to China, where he served as an adviser to Chiang Kai-shek and formed the Flying Tigers volunteer group to fight against the Japanese. Chennault found the much-storied group of misfits-turned-heroes well suited to his aggressive, unconventional personality. When America entered the war, the Flying Tigers were incorporated into Fourteenth Air Force, and Chennault was promoted to brigadier general and became its commander. Never on good terms with his Air Corps colleagues, Chennault persisted in infuriating his superiors by constantly complaining and circumventing the chain of command by dealing directly with Chiang and President Roosevelt. Consequently, George Marshall thought him disloyal and unreliable, Hap Arnold considered him a "crackpot," and Joe Stilwell (his superior in China) termed him "a jackass."

Even if his strategic theories had been correct, his method of promoting them ensured their demise. In fact, his ideas were not sound. He believed that a small force of aircraft, mostly pursuit with a handful of bombers, could so disrupt enemy logistics that it would lead to Japan's eventual defeat. But interdiction campaigns do not win wars, and it is doubtful that any amount of tactical airpower could have prevented Japan from overrunning China, much less brought about its defeat. Although he was an outstanding tactician whose determination in the face of overwhelming supply and equipment difficulties kept Fourteenth Air Force in the field, one can only classify Chennault's strategic ideas as puerile. Nevertheless, Byrd's book is excellent—the best available on this important airman.

A step below Byrd's effort is Jack Samson's *Chennault* (Garden City, N.Y.: Doubleday, 1987). Samson, who flew in the Fourteenth during the war and afterwards often went fishing and hunting with his former boss, provides some useful insights into Chennault's personality as well as a fairly detailed account of combat operations. Relying heavily on Chennault's personal papers (located at Stanford University), the book recounts the voluminous correspondence between the general and Chinese leaders. In addition, Samson covers the decade after the war, when Chennault organized the Civil Air Transport (CAT) company—especially interesting because CAT worked closely with the Central Intelligence Agency (CIA) and eventually became Air America, an airline secretly owned by the CIA. Unfortunately, the author's portrayal of Chennault is far too laudatory, glorifying the general throughout and depicting those who disagreed with him—Clayton Bissell, Stilwell, and Marshall—as uninformed, narrow-minded, and self-serving. A work of similar quality is Daniel Ford's *Flying Tigers: Claire Chennault and the American Volunteer Group* (Washington, D.C.: Smithsonian Institution Press, 1991).

Sam Mims's *Chennault of the Flying Tigers* (Philadelphia: Macrae-Smith, 1943) is a piece of wartime propaganda and a boys' adventure story. Books of only slightly higher caliber include Keith Ayling's *Old Leatherface of the Flying Tigers: The Story of General Chennault* (Indianapolis: The Bobbs-Merrill Co., 1945); Robert B. Hotz's *With General Chennault: The Story of the Flying Tigers* (1980; reprint, Washington, D.C.: Zenger Publishing Co., Inc.); and Duane P. Schultz's *The Maverick War: Chennault and the Flying Tigers* (New York: St. Martin's Press, 1987). Robert L. Scott's *Flying Tiger: Chennault of China* (Garden City, N.Y.: Doubleday, 1959) is interesting because Scott was a successful fighter pilot (author of *God Is My Co-Pilot*) and therefore speaks with some authority regarding Chennault's tactical ideas and his early-warning network. A pamphlet published by the Fourteenth Air Force Association and edited by Malcolm Rosholt, *Claire L. Chennault: A Tribute* (Rosholt, Wis., 1983), provides some interesting insights into Chennault's personality and leadership traits. Anna Chennault, the general's Chinese wife, whom he married in 1946, has also written two books that show a more personal side of the Flying Tiger, depicting him as kind, loving, romantic, and stubborn: *A Thousand Springs: The Biography of a Marriage* (New York: P. S. Eriksson, 1962) and *Chennault and the Flying Tigers* (New York: P. S. Eriksson, 1963). In addition, the books contain information from Chennault's early career that he presumably related to her during their marriage.

The title of Chennault's memoirs—*Way of a Fighter,* ed. Robert Hotz (New York: G. P. Putnam's Sons, 1949)—sums up the general's view of his life—an endless stream of battles against incompetent superiors. The foreword decries the situation then present in China, which he maintains resulted from the ineptitude of Stilwell and Marshall. In other words, Chennault has some old scores to settle in this memoir. No one emerges looking very dignified in this account of constant bickering; indeed, one is left with the impression that Washington very cleverly sent its most difficult senior officers to a minor theater, where they could fight amongst themselves and stay out of the way. The book's saving grace is its detailed account of fighter tactics used against the Japanese and the hardships of operating in the Chinese theater at the end of the American supply line.

**James H. "Jimmy" Doolittle's** racing-plane exploits, the Doolittle Raiders' "30 seconds over Tokyo" fame, and the fact that he lived well into his 90s probably made him America's best-known airman. A number of authors have written biographies about him, including several by Carroll Glines, who ghosted Doolittle's autobiography near the end of the general's life. Despite the copious amount of ink spilled on the general, we have yet to see a serious study that looks closely at his career and its effect on American airpower. Doolittle, one of the pioneers of instrument flying and advanced technology, was also an outstanding combat leader, commanding the Twelfth, Fifteenth, and

Eighth Air Forces during World War II. Yet, no one has addressed the issue of Doolittle's beliefs on the proper employment of air-power other than simply stating it should not be used as a tactical weapon. Surely, Doolittle must have held some strong opinions on what German target system was most important and vulnerable to Allied attack. Even the issue of Doolittle's stand regarding the oil-plan-versus-rail-plan controversy of 1944—an issue of enormous strategic importance—has evaded examination. In short, the definitive Doolittle biography has not yet appeared. Attempts include Lowell Thomas and Edward Jablonski's *Doolittle: A Biography* (Garden City, N.Y.: Doubleday, 1976); Carroll V. Glines's *Jimmy Doolittle: Daredevil Aviator and Scientist* (New York: Macmillan, 1972) and *Jimmy Doolittle, Master of the Calculated Risk* (New York: Van Nostrand Reinhold Co., 1980); Carl Mann's *Lightning in the Sky: The Story of Jimmy Doolittle* (New York: McBride, 1944); and Quentin Reynolds's *The Amazing Mr. Doolittle: A Biography of Lieutenant General James H. Doolittle* (New York: Appleton-Century-Crofts, 1953).

Unfortunately, his autobiography, *I Could Never Be So Lucky Again* (New York: Bantam Books, 1991), recounts the same anecdotes told elsewhere and offers no new insights into the man. The book does not offer a frank appraisal of Doolittle's effectiveness as a combat commander and fails to discuss key strategic issues such as the choice of industrial targets in Germany, the morality of strategic bombing, the development of the long-range escort fighter, and command relationships among senior Allied leaders.

**Ira C. Eaker,** another of the great pioneer airmen, met Arnold and Carl A. Spaatz at Rockwell Field, California, in 1918, and the three became friends and colleagues for life. One of the premier pilots between the wars, Eaker participated in the Pan American flight of 1926–27 and piloted the *Question Mark,* a Fokker C-2A, in the record-breaking air-refueling flight of

1929. He was also politically well connected, serving not only as an aide to Maj Gen James Fechet, the Air Corps chief, but also as the private pilot of Gen Douglas MacArthur. An excellent writer with a graduate degree in journalism, he figured prominently in airpower public-relations efforts during the 1930s and coauthored several aviation books with Hap Arnold. During World War II, he joined Spaatz in England to head VIII Bomber Command and, eventually, Eighth Air Force. In early 1944, Eaker moved down to Italy to command Mediterranean Allied Air Forces. James Parton, Eaker's aide through much of the war, tells this story in *"Air Force Spoken Here": General Ira Eaker and the Command of the Air* (Bethesda, Md.: Adler & Adler, 1986).

Fortunately for the country but perhaps unfortunately for Eaker, the task of organizing and standing up the Eighth proved extremely daunting, requiring his talents as a leader and manager. Strategic bombing had yet to prove itself; the green Eighth would enter combat against a battle-tested enemy; and the prodigious production capacity of America had not yet manifested itself. Moreover, just as the Eighth appeared strong enough to play a major role in the war against Germany, it was stripped of men and machines for operations in North Africa and then Italy. Arnold badgered Eaker unmercifully to do more yet at the same time throttled the resources necessary to do so. In what many (including Eaker himself) considered a "kick upstairs," Eaker received a promotion and moved to Italy, while Jimmy Doolittle took his place at the Eighth. Soon after, Eaker's labors bore fruit: the Allies established air superiority over the Luftwaffe, the invasion of France took place, and the sweep across northern Europe began, which eventually led to victory.

Parton relates Eaker's trials and challenges very well. Because he participated in the events of which he writes, he has a familiarity with the people and issues possessed by few other authors. And because he has a flair for history, he understands the context and significance of those issues. The main objection to his book is its unabashed admiration of Eaker. Apparently, the only mistakes the general ever made resulted from his intense loyalty to his subordinates or superiors—a weakness that many would perceive as strength of character. For whatever reason, it was clear by the end of the war that Eaker would not receive consideration for a fourth star (although he eventually got one, in 1985). Evidently, something in his performance or personality led Arnold, Spaatz, and Stuart Symington (the first Air Force secretary) to look elsewhere. After retiring, Eaker became a wealthy businessman and a prolific writer on airpower matters. Admiration aside, *"Air Force Spoken Here"* is an extremely well written and well researched book about a very important airman.

**Carl A. Spaatz** was the top American air commander of World War II; indeed, both Dwight Eisenhower and Omar Bradley rated him the best combat leader in the European theater. After the war, he became the first chief of staff of the newly independent Air Force. Two authors have written excellent biographies of this important airman. In *Master of Airpower: General Carl A. Spaatz* (Novato, Calif.: Presidio Press, 1988), David R. Mets of the School of Advanced Airpower Studies, Maxwell AFB, Alabama, relies heavily on the voluminous Spaatz papers in the Library of Congress as well as dozens of interviews, but the general's personality remains somewhat elusive. Mets provides a survey of the evolution of American airpower through World War II rather than an in-depth look at the man who mastered the new air weapon.

*Master of Airpower* portrays Spaatz as a "doer," a problem solver who achieved results, and an outstanding pilot who shot down three German aircraft in World War I (for which he won the Distinguished Service Cross) and flew aboard the *Question Mark* in 1929. When war broke out in Europe in 1939, Spaatz became the Air Corps's chief planner and then moved to England to command Eighth Air Force in 1942, Northwest African Air Force in 1943, and US Strategic Air Forces (USSTAF) in Europe in 1944. He was perhaps the only man whom Hap Arnold totally trusted—Eisenhower also held him in high regard. Although he compiled a very thorough piece of scholarship, Mets had trouble with his sponsors, who insisted upon removing much material considered either "too personal" or insufficiently complimentary towards Spaatz and the Air Force. The result is a somewhat impersonal portrait that glosses over some of the controversial issues in which Spaatz played such a major role.

Spaatz's other biographer, Richard G. Davis, wrote *Carl A. Spaatz and the Air War in Europe* (Washington, D.C.: Office of Air Force History, 1993), an outstanding effort. Unlike Mets, Davis did not write a full-length biography but concentrated on Spaatz's activities during World War II. The result is an extremely detailed, exhaustively researched, balanced, and quite readable account. Some of the issues examined in especially effective fashion include the North African invasion and the difficulties experienced in command and control ($C^2$) of air assets; Army Field Manual 100-20, *Command and Employment of Air Power*, the "Magna Carta" of airpower, which proclaimed airpower the equal of ground power; Spaatz's error in not recognizing the importance of long-range escort aircraft; the momentous Casablanca conference of January 1943 and its impact on air operations; the bombing assault on the island of Pantelleria (Italy) that resulted in surrender without requiring an invasion; Eaker's transfer to the Mediterranean and Doolittle's assumption of command at Eighth Air Force; the thorny command relationships among senior Allied leaders prior to the Normandy invasion; the controversy surrounding the rail and oil plans in early 1944; and the use of strategic bombers in a tactical role during the campaign in France. The book also includes excellent maps, organizational charts, and statistical appendices.

In addition, Davis provides a particularly good discussion of the attack on Dresden, Germany, in February 1945. This has always been a contentious issue because of the number of lives lost, the lateness of the war, and the cultural significance of the city. Davis concludes that the city was a legitimate military target, that the AAF did attempt to precisely bomb the city's marshaling yards, and that if opprobrium attaches to anyone it should be Winston Churchill, who specifically requested the bombing of east German cities to create refugees and spread havoc. Interestingly, although he claims that Dresden was an unfortunate victim of circumstance, Davis argues that such was not the case for Berlin. He maintains that Spaatz placed the German capital in a different category, ordering attacks on "city center" and employing the maximum number of incendiary bombs. As a result, USSTAF's attacks on Berlin were largely indistinguishable from the area attacks of Bomber Command.

Overall, Davis provides much detail and excellent insight into how Spaatz led and managed the American air effort in Europe as well as how he increased the magnitude of air attacks and made them both efficient and effective at destroying assigned targets. If the book has a shortcoming, it is Davis's inability to explain clearly how Spaatz and his staff selected targets, what specific effect they were trying to achieve (collapse of morale, revolt, decrease in production, loss of fighting spirit at the front, etc.), and how they measured success. Davis argues strenuously that oil was the key target and that Spaatz was correct in singling it out, but he provides no cogent logic or analysis to support this contention. Nevertheless, *Carl A. Spaatz and the Air War in Europe* is an outstanding book—perhaps the best, though partial, biography of an airman written to date. It sets a high standard by which other biographies should be measured.

**Laurence S. Kuter,** one of the more accomplished air planners and staff officers in Air Force history, served on the ACTS faculty from 1935 to 1939. A staunch advocate of strategic bombardment, he was one of four officers tasked in 1941 to write Air War Plans Division (AWPD) 1, *Munitions Requirements of the Army Air Force,* the seminal war plan that served as the blueprint for the air assault on Germany. Promotion followed quickly. The youngest general officer in the Army in 1942, he served on the War Department staff and Arnold's staff, commanded a bomb wing in England, served as deputy commander of the

Northwest African Tactical Air Force, and then returned to Washington for the rest of the war, even representing the AAF at the Yalta conference in 1945 during Arnold's illness. After the war, he again served on the Air Staff, headed the Military Air Transport Service during the Berlin airlift, commanded Air University and then Pacific Air Forces, and completed his career as a full general and commander of North American Air Defense Command (NORAD). Kuter, along with his wife, had a deep sense of history and left behind an astounding collection of scrapbooks and papers covering his entire career. Located in the Special Collections Branch of the Air Force Academy library in Colorado, this archive gives a remarkable picture of life in the Air Corps during the 1930s and sheds light on all other facets of the Air Force over a 40-year period.

Kuter's collection includes an autobiography that covers his life up to mid-1943, including his stay at West Point, service as a junior officer in a flying squadron, the hectic days in Washington at the start of World War II, and some very interesting character sketches of contemporary airmen who would later achieve high rank. Interestingly, his somewhat controversial personality comes through in these pages. For example, his extremely rapid promotion raised many eyebrows in the AAF. Additionally, since he was a trenchant observer, Arnold often sent him on troubleshooting tours around the world. But few local commanders liked what he reported back to Arnold. Consequently, many airmen viewed Kuter with a mixture of fear, awe, and resentment. Unfortunately, Kuter did not complete this most interesting 300-page memoir.

Because of Hap Arnold's illness—one of his several heart attacks—Kuter, then a major general, was selected to attend the Allied conference at Yalta in February 1945 as the AAF representative. Kuter tells this story in *Airman at Yalta* (New York: Duell, Sloan, and Pearce, 1955). However, the book's title does not accurately describe its contents, most of which covers the preliminary meetings in Britain and on Malta prior to the main event in the Crimea. Barely 10 percent of the book actually deals with Yalta, and much of that addresses unimportant protocol details. Moreover, the actual air discussions between Kuter and representatives from the Royal Air Force (RAF) and the Red Air Force proved completely fruitless. The Americans had hoped to establish a communication system to coordinate the air efforts of the three countries and thus avoid the danger of fratricide. In addition, the United States pushed for an agreement to locate B-29 bases near Vladivostok for the purpose of bombing Japan. Because the war in Europe was ending, however, the Soviets had little incentive to be agreeable and rejected both proposals. Overall, *Airman at Yalta* misses badly, containing few real insights into air strategy and spending too much time describing the fare at the seemingly endless stream of formal dinners during the conference.

**George C. Kenney,** America's top airman in the Pacific theater during World War II, had served as a fighter pilot in World War I, downing two German aircraft and winning the Distinguished Service Cross. Between the wars, he attended Command and General Staff College and the Army War College and then taught at ACTS. He also earned a reputation as an accomplished engineer through assignments at Wright Field, Ohio, and became recognized as an expert in tactical aviation. Significantly, while serving as an air attaché to Paris during the German invasion of France in 1940, he witnessed the effectiveness of airpower in that campaign. Soon after Pearl Harbor, Arnold selected Kenney as MacArthur's air deputy. For the rest of the war, the short, fiery, and tireless Kenney served as commander of Fifth Air Force and then Far East Air Forces (FEAF) under the difficult and demanding MacArthur. His achieved dramatic success in such battles as Bismarck Sea, Rabaul, Wewak, and the Philippine campaign and has become the prototype for the modern concept of an "air component commander"—the individual in charge of all aviation assets in a theater. Because Kenney had an outstanding grasp of what is today called "operational art" and of how airpower could be used to complement the operations of land and sea forces, many people considered him the most ac-

complished combat air strategist of the war. In April 1945, he became a full general—one of only four American airmen holding
that rank during the war. However, he never seemed to hold
Arnold's complete confidence, as did Spaatz, and when B-29s arrived in the Pacific theater at the end of 1944, they were not assigned to Kenney but were commanded directly from Washington. This attitude was reinforced after the war when Spaatz
succeeded Arnold and was confirmed when Hoyt Vandenberg—
nine years younger than Kenney—replaced Spaatz as chief of
staff in 1948. Instead, Kenney became commander of the new
Strategic Air Command (SAC) after the war, but because he
seemed more interested in dabbling in politics, he performed
poorly. When the Berlin crisis of 1948 broke out, Vandenberg
conducted an investigation of SAC's war readiness. The results
were unacceptable, so he relieved Kenney and replaced him with
Curtis LeMay. Kenney then assumed command of Air University,
retiring from that position in 1951.

Kenney wrote one of the more interesting memoirs of the
war, *General Kenney Reports: A Personal History of the Pacific
War* (1949; reprint, Washington, D.C.: Air Force History and
Museums Program, 1997), which clearly reveals his aggressive
and somewhat flamboyant personality. The book makes apparent Kenney's popularity with both his subordinates and
MacArthur. Believing that a commander's first responsibility
was to his troops, Kenney worked hard to ensure that his men
had adequate housing and food but also recognized that
largely intangible factors such as pride and recognition of a job
well done were the greatest motivators. In addition, because
the Southwest Pacific was considered a minor theater compared to Europe and even the Central Pacific, Kenney had to
improvise, doing more with less throughout the war. He had
the remarkable ability to squeeze effective combat results out
of a small force at the end of a 10,000-mile supply line.

The book also reveals Kenney's ideas on airpower employment.
First and foremost, he believed in air superiority. Repeatedly, he
lectured MacArthur and other surface commanders on the need
to destroy Japanese airpower and then establish bases within
range of projected Allied operations. At the same time, he made
his mark as an ingenious and clever tactical innovator, largely

responsible for such successes as the combat use of the parafrag bomb, skip-bombing techniques, and "commerce destroyers"—B-25s armed with eight machine guns and heavy cannons for use against enemy ships. On the other hand, this ability as a tactician made him suspect among strategic-bombing advocates like Arnold. When B-29s were due to arrive in-theater in late 1944, Kenney argued that they would be most effective against Japanese targets in the East Indies, such as oil refineries, and would thus assist MacArthur in his drive northward. Arnold, however, wanted the heavy bombers to strike directly at Japanese industry in the home islands, not in an interdiction campaign supporting the Army. In a sense, Kenney's close relationship with MacArthur thus negatively affected his standing within the AAF, which experienced further erosion due to Kenney's forays into presidential politics. In April 1943, Kenney met with Sen. Arthur Vandenberg (the general's uncle) of Michigan, one of the leading Republicans in the country, to discuss MacArthur's presidential candidacy in 1944. Arnold undoubtedly knew of these discussions and would not have welcomed them. As a consequence, when Twentieth Air Force went to the Pacific, Arnold took the unprecedented step of commanding it personally from Washington. After the German surrender, Arnold still did not grant control of the B-29s to Kenney but sent Spaatz to the Pacific as commander of all strategic air units.

Certainly, Kenney's calculated efforts to portray himself as the ragged, rugged warrior who worked hard, played hard, and got results in the face of adversity wear a bit thin as the book progresses. His overtly racist statements—such as "Nips are just vermin to be exterminated"—are also jarring to modern ears. In addition, Kenney's unalloyed affection for and admiration of MacArthur and all his works give the impression that one is reading a press release for the famous general. Despite his shortcomings, Kenney proved himself an outstanding combat commander, and *General Kenney Reports* gives readers a wonderful view of the unique difficulties encountered in the Pacific war. Airpower played an enormously important role in this theater, and the book clearly demonstrates Kenney's part in its success. It is must reading for all airmen.

The only biography of Kenney to date is *MacArthur's Airman: General George C. Kenney and the Air War in the Southwest Pacific* (Lawrence, Kans.: University Press of Kansas, 1998) by Col Thomas E. Griffith Jr. This excellent study begins with Kenney's early experiences as an observation pilot in World War I and follows his career during the interwar years. Most of the book concentrates on Kenney's activities during the war—specifically, how he exploited airpower's advantages to accomplish MacArthur's strategic objectives. It also investigates Kenney's problems in balancing MacArthur's demands with Arnold's, as well as those of the commanders of the ground and naval forces within his theater. Griffith concludes that part of Kenney's success lay in his flexible use of airpower, both operationally and organizationally. His capacity to innovate and make do with meager resources seemed endless. Nevertheless, although Kenney was a brilliant theater air commander, he had little appreciation for the strategic problems facing Arnold. This attitude caused tension between the two men, and their relationship appreciably worsened during the war.

Integrating a wide variety of primary and secondary sources, Griffith has produced an excellent, in-depth study of Kenney's contribution to the war. Of particular note is his focus on the role of intelligence and logistics—specifically, aircraft and engine maintenance—in Kenney's success. Traditionally, historians of airpower have paid little attention to these areas, despite their crucial importance to winning the air war. Griffith presents a balanced account, not averse to criticizing Kenney when appropriate. As a result, he notes Kenney's anti-Navy parochialism, which did little to foster smooth relations in the Pacific, as well as his tendency to exaggerate his command's accomplishments. In addition, despite Kenney's predilection for tactical airpower, he considered interdiction more important than close air support, which caused some problems with ground commanders. Unfortunately, *MacArthur's Airman* ends at the conclusion of the war and does not follow through on Kenney's postwar career. As a result, we still have no good analysis of why Kenney succeeded so well in the war but failed so miserably as SAC's first commander. We can only hope that Griffith will soon extend his study to tell this important story as well.

**Donald Wilson** played a relatively minor role in World War II, serving as George Kenney's chief of staff for nearly two years. More importantly in some respects, he also served as an instructor at ACTS in the early 1930s, when American airpower doctrine was being codified. Wilson tells his story in his privately printed and somewhat eccentric memoirs *Wooing Peponi: My Odyssey thru Many Years* (Carmel, Calif.: Angel Press, 1973). Fancying himself a philosopher, Wilson includes discussions on life, education, politics, war strategy, and automobiles. (Incidentally, *peponi* is allegedly a Swahili term for paradise, so Wilson's book chronicles his search for it.) Unfortunately, the coverage of his years at ACTS is self-serving and egotistical: Wilson claims sole credit for devising the doctrine used by the AAF in World War II, and he is obviously quite irritated at not having received due credit for his ideas. On the other hand, his description of military life during the interwar years is very interesting—the frequent moves, the often spartan living conditions, the camaraderie and naïveté bordering on childishness exhibited by early aviators regarding weather and navigation techniques, and so forth. It is truly amazing how many Air Corps pilots crash-landed or were lost because they forgot their maps, followed railroad tracks into box canyons, or failed to check the weather before takeoff. Wilson therefore provides an interesting portrait of a bygone age.

**Kenneth N. Walker,** another of the major players in the formulation of doctrine at ACTS, served as a bombardment instructor during the crucial years from 1929 to 1934. Walker epitomized the strategic thinkers at the school, and his famous statement in one of his lectures set the tone for their beliefs: "The well-organized, well-planned, and well-flown air force attack will constitute an offensive that cannot be stopped." He pushed this theory with a vehemence and stubbornness that rivaled

Chennault's contrary point of view. The AAF benefited and suffered from the attitudes and personalities of both men.

In August 1941, Walker and three colleagues (Hal George, Larry Kuter, and Haywood "Possum" Hansell) put together AWPD-1. Soon after, Walker was sent to the Pacific. Kenney wanted Walker as his bomb commander because of his intensity and single-mindedness. Indeed, the tireless Walker drove himself so hard that Kenney feared he would snap and have to be sent home. Instead, contrary to orders, Walker led a bombing strike on Rabaul on 5 January 1943 and was shot down. For his courage and self-sacrifice, he received the Medal of Honor posthumously.

Martha Byrd, Chennault's most successful biographer, wrote a manuscript that outlines Walker's short but significant career but died before completing it. She left behind a readable portrait of a driven man—not only an accomplished and dedicated professional but also a vain, ambitious, and inflexible individual. However, Byrd's study lacks a contextual basis that explains fully the role of doctrine, ACTS's part in formulating doctrine, and Walker's influence at the school. In addition, Byrd did not adequately flesh out her subject's tour at V Bomber Command. The opening year of the Pacific air war was plagued by shortages of men and materiel, and the overall strategy for defeating Japan had not yet become clear. Walker's role in those crucial months, therefore, could have been pivotal and needs further exploration.

Air University Press has edited Byrd's manuscript and added a chapter written by David R. Mets to provide the requisite context. *Kenneth N. Walker: Airpower's Untempered Crusader,* which appeared in the spring of 1997, is well worth the wait.

**Haywood S. Hansell Jr.,** another man who taught strategic bombardment theory at ACTS and later served as a planner and commander in World War II, joined the Air Corps in 1928. After flying for five years, "Possum," as he was known to his friends, attended ACTS as a student and remained there as a faculty member. Although he joined the "bomber clique" at Maxwell Field, Alabama,

41

he was also an excellent fighter pilot, and Claire Chennault chose him as a member of his acrobatic team. When war broke out in Europe, Hansell joined the Air Staff and set up the air-intelligence section. In August 1941, he joined three other officers in writing AWPD-1. The following year, he played a major role in updating this plan—AWPD-42, *Requirements for Air Ascendancy*—while also serving as a bomb-division commander in Eighth Air Force. After the Casablanca conference of January 1943, Hansell drew up a plan for the Combined Bomber Offensive. Thus, he played a key role in all three of the major strategic air plans used against Germany.

After Hansell's return to the Air Staff in Washington, Arnold formed Twentieth Air Force, consisting of the first operational B-29s. Although stationed thousands of miles away, Arnold chose to command the Twentieth himself—to keep the new bombers out of the unenlightened hands of the Army and Navy commanders in the Pacific. Hansell became chief of staff of the Twentieth, but because of Arnold's other duties and his chronically poor health, Hansell became de facto commander of the new air force. His role became more direct in October 1944, when he went to the Mariana Islands to head XXI Bomber Command. His position there seemed almost hopeless. The new B-29s were having severe teething troubles—the weather was abysmal, the distances were enormous, the supply lines were slow and sporadic, and all the while Arnold issued impatient demands for greater results. In an attempt to spur Hansell to more creative tactics that would produce greater damage to the Japanese war industry, Arnold advised him to abandon his attempts at high-altitude precision bombing and opt for low-level area attacks that employed incendiaries. But Hansell resisted. His patience—never copious in the best of circumstances—at an end, Arnold relieved Hansell in January 1945 and replaced him with Curtis LeMay. Hansell returned to the United States, served briefly as a base commander in Arizona, and retired in 1946. He was recalled to active duty during the Korean War and promoted to major general, serving first as chief of mobilization on the Air Staff and then as the senior airman on the Weapons Systems Evaluation Group. He retired again in 1955.

Hansell tells his life in two privately printed volumes. The first, *The Air Plan That Defeated Hitler* (1972; reprint, Washington,

D.C.: Government Printing Office, 1975), relates his years at ACTS and then his combat experience in Europe. The second volume, *Strategic Air War against Japan* (Maxwell AFB, Ala.: Air War College, Airpower Research Institute, 1980), covers Hansell's experiences as chief of staff of Twentieth Air Force and then as commander of XXI Bomber Command. (In 1986 the Office of Air Force History revised and combined these two volumes into *The Strategic Air War against Germany and Japan: A Memoir* [Washington, D.C.].) Hansell believed passionately in the concept of the daylight, strategic, precision bombing of industrial systems. He helped formulate and then implement this doctrine in war, remaining committed to it even when certain aspects proved wanting. Significantly, Hansell argues that a sustained air attack could have brought Germany to its knees prior to Operation Overlord, but "diversions" constantly thrown in the path of Eighth Air Force (e.g., the battle against the submarine; the invasions of North Africa, then Sicily, then Italy, then Normandy; and the destruction of the German V-1 and V-2 rocket sites) prevented the execution of this concentrated campaign. But this is a politically naive view. The Battle of the Atlantic and the destruction of the rocket sites were strategic requirements of the first order. Our closest ally was in dire straits—we had to act. In addition, airpower was absolutely essential if any of these amphibious landings were to succeed; troops could not be left on the beaches to be slaughtered. Although Hansell questions the utility of such landings, he forgets the life-and-death struggle occurring on the Eastern Front. Stalin demanded a second front, and the fate of the Grand Alliance—and thus ultimate victory—depended on Britain and the United States opening such a front.

Nevertheless, Hansell's is one of the most articulate accounts of the development of strategic-bombing doctrine and practice. One can argue with his postulates and conclusions, but the arguments remain clear and stark. These books are the best defense of American airpower doctrine during World War II yet written.

Charles R. Griffith, Hansell's only biographer, wrote *The Quest: Haywood Hansell and American Strategic Bombing in World War II* (Maxwell AFB, Ala.: Air University Press, 1999), a much needed revision of the author's PhD dissertation at the

University of Tennessee. Griffith achieves more balance than in his earlier effort and is more willing to admit some of Hansell's mistakes. However, he still relies far too heavily on a few secondary sources (mostly the official history), Hansell's memoirs, and interviews with family members. He employs almost no archival material to examine the assumptions behind AWPD-1 and AWPD-42—or Hansell's role in shaping American strategy in the Combined Bomber Offensive. Clearly, Griffith feels that Hansell suffered at the hands of several colleagues— Arnold, LeMay, Larry Norstad, and Emmett "Rosie" O'Donnell—who simply did not understand airpower. Griffith acknowledges that Hansell was too inflexible in his thinking and that this intransigence contained the seeds of his downfall. Importantly, the author also makes a moral argument for Hansell's rigid adherence to the doctrine that he helped formulate. This is a useful discussion that the author could have expanded to deal more rigorously with arguments for and against the B-29 campaign against Japan. Griffith admits that Hansell's tactics were not successful, whereas LeMay's certainly were—at least according to the Strategic Bombing Survey. Moreover, Hansell seems to have disagreed with the decision to drop the atomic bombs on Japan, but the book contains no discussion of the implications of such dissent in terms of American, Allied, or Japanese lives saved or spent. In addition, Griffith does not cover Hansell's recall to duty and his service during the Korean War. Still, *The Quest* is a useful book about one of our great thinkers and planners.

Another of the largely forgotten figures of American airpower, **Ennis Whitehead** played an important role at an important time. Enlisting in the Army in 1917, Whitehead quickly joined the Air Service, won his wings, and went to France. An excellent flyer, he became a test pilot and thus saw no combat. After the war, his reputation as an aviator grew within the small coterie of military airmen: he participated in Billy Mitchell's bombing tests against the *Ost-*

*friesland* in 1921, joined the Pan American flight of 1927—narrowly escaping death in a midair collision over Buenos Aires—and set a speed record from Miami to Panama in 1931. When war came, he went to the Pacific, where he became George Kenney's strong right arm. Whitehead stayed in Asia for the next seven years, becoming commander of Fifth Air Force in 1944; after Kenney left the theater, he took over FEAF. Returning to the States in 1949, Whitehead commanded the short-lived Continental Air Command and then Air Defense Command until his retirement in 1951.

Donald M. Goldstein tells his story in "Ennis C. Whitehead: Aerospace Commander and Pioneer" (PhD diss., University of Denver, 1970). The author, who later edited the immensely popular histories begun by the late Gordon Prange, argues that Whitehead was a tactical genius and the brains behind such stunning air victories as Wewak, Rabaul, Gloucester, and Bismarck Sea. Additionally, although Kenney has received credit for such innovations as skip bombing, parafrag bombs, nose cannons in medium bombers, and the use of mass-troop transport, Goldstein argues that Whitehead actually pioneered them. His research is impressive, but Goldstein merely asserts his points rather than proves them. Unquestionably, Whitehead was an outstanding tactician who performed extremely well in the Southwest Pacific theater, but attempting to pinpoint credit is generally far more difficult than assigning blame. Victory does have a thousand fathers. Furthermore, Goldstein repeatedly states that Whitehead was an outstanding planner but does not explain precisely what this means: how did he actually go about the crucial business of determining objectives, allocating resources, anticipating enemy counters, and measuring results? Whitehead himself emerges in this portrait as a hard, uncompromising man with a heavy twinge of anti-Semitism and chauvinism; he was a good combat commander who engendered respect rather than admiration among his subordinates. Also, some members of the Air Force hierarchy thought him too attached to Kenney and MacArthur, too political, too outspoken, and too tactically focused. Whitehead was disgusted by the appointment of Vandenberg rather than Kenney as chief of staff in 1948 and was outraged when the new chief quickly relieved Kenney as commander of SAC. Reputedly, he also resented not being named vice chief of staff and not receiving a fourth star. These feelings, combined with ill health, caused him to tender his resignation in early 1951. Despite Goldstein's obvious and exaggerated affection for his subject, his dissertation is a very solid piece of scholarship.

One of the more well-traveled airmen of World War II, **Lewis H. Brereton** graduated from the Naval Academy, served on Billy Mitchell's staff during and after World War I, and rose steadily through the ranks in the years thereafter. At the time of Pearl Harbor, he was commander of FEAF—such as it was—under MacArthur. When that command collapsed a few months later, he went to Australia for a brief stay, to India to command Tenth Air Force, and thence to Egypt to head Ninth Air Force. In 1943 he took the Ninth to England in preparation for the Overlord invasion, and in August 1944 he was selected to lead the First Allied Airborne Army for Operation Market-Garden, an Anglo-American operation designed to secure bridges in Holland. After the war, Lieutenant General Brereton served as a senior military adviser to the Atomic Energy Commission until his retirement in 1948. He was a key figure in several important events of the war, including the destruction of his air force at Clark Field, Philippines; the fall of Burma; the British success at El Alamein, Egypt; the low-level strike on Ploesti, Romania, in August 1943; D day; and "a bridge too far" at Arnhem, Netherlands. He recounts his experiences in *The Brereton Diaries: The War in the Air in the Pacific, Middle East and Europe, 3 October 1941–8 May 1945* (New York: W. Morrow and Co., 1946).

Unfortunately, this account is not enlightening. Because Brereton tells us in the preface that he began thinking of publishing his diaries in 1942, we get the strong suspicion that he is writing not only after the event but also with an eye to how he would look in print sometime in the future. Frankly, the memoir contains much unimportant detail but little real insight into air strategy or command problems. For example, the text barely hints at severe personality conflicts between Allied leaders at the time of D day and fails to mention the enormous struggle over targeting priorities that occurred at the same time, which nearly caused both Eisenhower and Spaatz to resign in protest. Overall, *The Brereton Diaries* is an unsatisfactory account of little value.

A far more useful effort is a lengthy, two-part article written by Roger G. Miller, "A 'Pretty Damn Able Commander': Lewis Hyde Brereton," *Air Power History* 47 (Winter 2000): 4–27 and *Air Power History* 48 (Spring 2001): 22–45. Because Brereton left no papers and died over three decades ago, Miller had a difficult time researching his subject. Nevertheless, he sheds much light on Brereton's energetic and aggressive personality, as well as his shortcomings. Always better as an operator than as a staff officer or planner, Brereton emerges as a capable though not outstanding combat leader. Miller's discussion of Brereton's role in the initial days of World War II, when his forces were largely destroyed in short order by Japanese airpower, is especially good. Even so, he breaks off his story as Brereton is about to take Ninth Air Force to Europe in preparation for Overlord. In short, the story ends as we approach the climax of Brereton's career. Hopefully, Miller will continue his efforts to uncover this forgotten airman.

Like Brereton, **Hugh J. Knerr** was a graduate of the Naval Academy who transferred to the Army so he could be a pilot. Knerr made the change after three years, joining the Army in 1911 as an artillery officer and finally wrangling a pilot-training slot in 1917. Over the next two decades, he flew observation and bombardment aircraft while acquiring a reputation as an excellent administrator. As a result, after the formation of GHQ

Air Force in 1935, its commander, Frank Andrews, selected Knerr as his chief of staff. Unfortunately, because of his reputation as an outspoken advocate of strategic airpower, in 1939 he was banished to Fort Sam Houston in San Antonio, to the same position occupied by Billy Mitchell the previous decade. Knerr chose to retire, but when war broke out, he was brought back on active duty and sent to Europe as Eighth Air Force's deputy commander for administration. He retired again after the war, but due to a scandal involving a senior officer, he was activated once again in 1947 and became the first inspector general of the Air Force. He retired a third time in 1949.

Knerr wrote an unpublished memoir "The Vital Era, 1887–1950," now located in the Air Force Academy library's Special Collections Branch. In truth, this work is not overly useful, conveying no hint of the fire that drove Knerr out of the service on two occasions. Although he overtly supported Frank Andrews over Hap Arnold, the memoir fails to mention that affinity. Furthermore, he received praise for his outstanding work administering and supplying American bomber forces in England, but "The Vital Era" scarcely discusses how he achieved such successes. Instead, we have a barely interesting memoir of anecdotes, stories, and opinions that provide little insight or analysis.

One of the more noted tactical airmen in World War II, flamboyant and handsome **Elwood R. "Pete" Quesada** entered the Air Service in 1924 and, upon winning his wings, lived a most unusual life as a junior officer. He served as the personal pilot for the chief of the Air Corps; assistant secretary of war; secretary of war; George Marshall, when the future five-star was a colonel at Fort Benning, Georgia; and the ambassador to Cuba. Such activities made him politically well connected to an unusual degree and served him in good stead in the years ahead. In addition, in 1929 he joined Spaatz and Eaker on the famous *Question Mark* flight over San Diego.

After a stint on Arnold's staff, Quesada became commander of an air defense group on Long Island in July 1941. He took his group to North Africa in 1943 as a brigadier general and was soon named deputy commander of the Coastal Air Force, responsible for defending Allied ports against Luftwaffe attacks and interdicting enemy shipping in the Mediterranean. After some initial difficulties with his British superior, Quesada settled down and performed well. In late 1943, he went to England as head of IX Fighter Command to prepare for the Normandy invasion. For the three months prior to D day, his aircraft flew escort missions for the heavy bombers of Eighth Air Force and bombed bridges, rail yards, and enemy fortifications in western France. When the Allies landed, Quesada's fighter-bombers worked closely with ground forces in the drive across France and into Germany. His reputation grew, and by the end of the war, he had become a major general widely recognized as a tactical air expert. After the war, he took over Tactical Air Command (TAC) and received a third star. But in the financial austerity of the Truman era, Air Force leaders decided to downsize TAC, combining it with Air Defense Command to form Continental Air Command, thus nudging out Quesada. After a series of unremarkable assignments that included command of atomic-bomb tests at Eniwetok, Quesada retired in 1951, embittered by what he considered poor treatment by the Air Force.

The only biography of Quesada is Thomas Alexander Hughes's *Over Lord: General Pete Quesada and the Triumph of Tactical Air Power in World War II* (New York: Free Press, 1995). Although this study is wonderfully written and engaging, it appears that Hughes became too attached to his subject; moreover, his bias against strategic airpower tends to distort his story. Part of the problem lies in the common tendency of the biographer to inflate the role and importance of his subject while denigrating or ignoring the other players involved.

The truly fascinating question that Hughes does not adequately address is how Pete Quesada, with virtually no operational experience prior to the war and a stint in North Africa that focused on air defense and interdiction, could learn the intricacies of tactical air support so quickly and effectively. Regrettably, the author sheds little light on this transformation; instead, he portrays Quesada as a creative genius who pioneered a number of tactical devices that saw their first use in the months following D day. The truth is different. Other people devised most of the innovations Hughes lauds, but these airmen—Sir Arthur "Mary" Coningham and Sir John "Jack" Slessor of the RAF, Gen John "Joe" Cannon in North Africa and Italy, and Kenney in the Pacific—receive scarce mention and even less credit. These airmen introduced the concepts of air-ground radio communications and forward air controllers and collocated air and ground headquarters, all of which Quesada adopted in France. Also of concern is the author's treatment of Hoyt Vandenberg, Quesada's superior as commander of Ninth Air Force and as chief of staff after the war. Clearly, Quesada believed that he should have commanded the Ninth in the fall of 1944, not Vandenberg. Hughes's treatment of this relationship is not convincing.

Nevertheless, no one questions tactical airpower's status as a decisive factor in the Allied victory, and Pete Quesada remains a recognized expert in applying that weapon. Hughes has done a fine job of telling this vital story.

After an illustrious showing in World War II, **Hoyt S. Vandenberg** became Air Force chief of staff in 1948. In that position, he played an important role in the significant events of his time: the formation of SAC, unification of the armed services, formation of an independent air force, Berlin airlift, B-36/supercarrier controversy with the Navy, development of the hydrogen bomb, and Korean War. Graduating from West Point in 1923, Vandenberg served as a fighter pilot for the next decade, becoming one of the Air Corps's outstanding flyers. When war broke out in Europe, he was assigned to the Air Staff in Washington as an air planner for the North African and Normandy invasions; he also served as a diplomat in Moscow, chief of staff of Twelfth Air Force, deputy commander of Allied Expeditionary Air Forces, and commander of Ninth Air Force, the largest tactical air unit in history. After the war, Vandenberg returned to Washington where, after brief stints on the Air Staff and as the War Department's intelligence chief, President Harry S. Truman named him director of central intelligence. Returning to uniform in 1948, he became Spaatz's deputy and won a fourth star. When Spaatz retired, Vandenberg became chief of staff, a position he held for over five years.

In my book *Hoyt S. Vandenberg: The Life of a General* (1989; reprint, Washington, D.C.: Air Force History and Museums Program, 2000), I conclude that Vandenberg was an exceptionally well rounded officer: an outstanding pilot, accomplished planner and staff officer, effective commander, and a passable diplomat. Moreover, his appealing personality, one of his greatest strengths, helped him make more friends than enemies. In short, he embodied the superb blend of leader and manager that the new Air Force needed to get off the ground.

In retrospect, perhaps I underestimated his effectiveness as a member of the JCS. After I wrote this book, my tenure at the Air Staff showed me the extremely competitive environment that exists among the services. Consequently, I can now better understand the challenges facing an infant service led by such a youthful general. The fact that the Air Force not only survived but indeed thrived—receiving nearly half of the entire defense budget by 1953—is a clear tribute to Vandenberg's exceptional political and organizational skills.

Vandenberg is the subject of two dissertations: Jon A. Reynolds's "Education and Training for High Command: Hoyt S. Vandenberg's Early Career" (Duke University, 1980) and Robert L. Smith's "The Influence of USAF Chief of Staff General Hoyt S. Vandenberg on United States National Security Policy" (American University, 1965). Reynolds takes an interesting approach, studying the early career of a future general. Although little personal documentation remains from Vandenberg's early life, Reynolds examines in-depth the operational units to which Vandenberg was assigned during the interwar years. This approach, an invaluable foundation for my own study, allows Reynolds to construct a portrait of a junior officer's life during the Roaring Twenties and the Great Depression.

Smith (a political scientist, not a historian) concentrates on Vandenberg's tenure as chief, emphasizing his role in the formulation of national security policy. Relying heavily on congressional testimony, Smith concludes that Vandenberg was extremely effective in selling not only the public but also Congress on the idea of airpower as the first line of American defense.

**Orvil A. Anderson,** a minor figure who nevertheless played a role in some key events in airpower history, entered the Air Service during World War I and gained fame as one of the top balloonists in the country. In fact, he achieved an altitude record for balloons in 1935 that lasted for 22 years and which won him both the Harmon and Mackay trophies. After converting to airplanes and flying for several years, Anderson joined the Air Staff's Plans Division. In 1943 he moved to England to become the chief planner of Eighth Air Force; the following year, he became a major general and director of operations for the Eighth. As the war in Europe drew to a close, he assumed responsibilities as the senior military adviser to the US Strategic Bombing Survey for both the European and Pacific divisions. In this capacity, he had a number of heated arguments with the Navy over who played the more important role in the defeat of Japan. In late 1946, he became the first commandant of the new Air War College at Maxwell Field. Anderson had trouble controlling his temper and tongue, a problem that became painfully apparent in 1950. Soon after the outbreak of the Korean War, he told a newspaper reporter that the Soviet Union was clearly behind the invasion of South Korea and that, given the order, he would willingly wipe out Russia with atomic strikes within a week. Because MacArthur and the secretary of the Navy had made inappropriate statements only a few days before—earning rebukes from President Truman—Anderson's comments were especially inopportune. Within days he was relieved of his command and pushed into retirement. In the atomic age, loose cannons were most unwelcome. John H. Scrivner's "Pioneer into Space: A Biography of Major General Orvil Arson Anderson" (PhD diss., University of Oklahoma, 1971) relates the life of this outspoken airman who epitomized the "cold warriors" spawned in the aftermath of World War II. Scrivner's is a sympathetic and workmanlike account of a man whose retirement was in some ways more important than his career.

**Howard A. Craig,** another solid and dependable airman who entered the service during World War I, stuck with it through the lean years of the next two decades, rose to high rank during World War II, and then helped shape the new era and the new Air Force that followed. Known as "Pinky" throughout his career, Craig was a bomber pilot during the interwar years—he participated in Mitchell's bombing of the battleships in 1923—and in 1941 joined the Air War Plans Division in Washington. He helped plan the North African invasion, staying on to command a fighter group in Tunisia. Returning to the Air Staff in 1943, he led the Operations and Requirements Division and then moved to the War Department's general staff, where he won a second star. After the war, he headed Alaskan Command for two years—a difficult tour marked by harsh operational conditions and low priority—and became a lieutenant general. In 1947 Craig was named deputy chief of staff for materiel in the new Air Force. Following a brief stint as inspector general, he assumed command of the National War College in 1952, retiring from that position in 1955.

After Craig's death, Dale L. Walker edited the general's memoirs, published as *Sunward I've Climbed: A Personal Narrative of Peace and War* (El Paso, Tex.: Texas Western Press, 1975). Like many such efforts written late in life, Craig recalls his earlier experiences more clearly and more fondly than the later ones. In this case, such recollection is a plus because the author's memories of his life as a junior officer are both interesting and entertaining. In 1909 he saw his first aircraft on the beach at Atlantic City; the pilot, who actually offered him a free ride, was the noted pioneer aviator Walter Brookins. Craig was bitten by the aviation bug that summer and never recovered. His account of life in the Air Corps is one of the best portraits of garrison life in peacetime, relating a disturbing number of plane crashes brought on by poorly maintained and outmoded equipment and by insufficient training. Missing, however, is a discussion of the many problems faced by the new Air Force after it achieved independence in 1947. Nevertheless, the memoirs of Pinky Craig, not one of our more famous airmen but a reliable and highly capable professional who served his country well, are certainly worth reading.

**Dale O. Smith** graduated from West Point in 1934 and attended flying school. Too big to fit comfortably into fighters (he was six feet, seven inches tall), Smith flew bombers most of his career. At the outbreak of World War II, he was a B-17 squadron commander, and for more than a year he hunted German submarines in the Atlantic. In late 1943, he joined Eighth Air Force in England as a bomb-group commander and flew 31 combat missions. Following this tour, he returned to the Pentagon and after the war served on the faculty of the Air War College. In the 1950s, Smith served as chief negotiator with the Saudi Arabians regarding basing rights in the peninsula and then became an air division commander on Okinawa. In 1961, now a major general, Smith became special assistant for arms control to the JCS; two years later, he moved to the Joint Strategic Survey Council, retiring from that position in 1964.

A gifted writer, Smith published two partial memoirs and a book on strategy; he also coauthored another work on defense policy with Curtis LeMay. His *Cradle of Valor: The Intimate Letters of a Plebe at West Point between the Two World Wars* (Chapel Hill, N.C.: Algonquin Books of Chapel Hill, 1988), a collection of letters between Smith and his family during his first year as a cadet, includes detailed explanations of everything from daily routines, conduct at the dining table, athletics, drill, the cadet honor code, and relations (very few) with the opposite sex. The book includes some wonderful and touching insights and stories, but few readers other than academy graduates will find it interesting.

Smith's *Screaming Eagle: Memoirs of a B-17 Group Commander* (Chapel Hill, N.C.: Algonquin Books of Chapel Hill, 1990) recounts his combat experiences during World War II. The confusion and unpredictability of war emerge as one of the book's dominant themes. We see these elements in the unreliable weather that closed landing fields and caused crash landings and midair collisions; in the tired mechanics who installed an engine part incorrectly, causing an in-flight fire; and in the constant surprises of the enemy, who never fought at the time, place, or in the manner expected.

In November 1943, Smith assumed command of the hard-luck 384th Bomb Group, based at the English village of Grafton Underwood in Northamptonshire. Smith had the task of whipping this B-17 unit, reputedly the worst in Eighth Air Force, into shape, restoring its morale, and, more importantly, improving its performance. He began by setting strict discipline and training requirements. Although his initial attempts were met with apathy or downright resentment, Smith persevered, and within a year he had transformed the 384th into one of the top combat air units in Europe. This highly personal book—as was his work on his cadet experiences—also recounts the author's failing marriage to a woman worn down by a war that continually kept her man away. Such a story, familiar though it is, has seldom been told more objectively and understandingly. *Screaming Eagle* is well written, well conceived, and well balanced. Smith is forthright about his many mistakes and errors of judgment as both a leader and a man. He has no axes to grind or darts to hurl. Instead, he simply tells the story of a professional soldier who, like countless others, did his best under very trying circumstances.

**Frank Armstrong** had the distinction of serving as the model for Brig Gen Frank Savage in the best-selling novel, movie, and television series *Twelve O'Clock High*. Although a professional baseball player, he gave up the diamond for the cockpit in 1929. He flew a variety of aircraft over the next decade and in 1942 joined Eighth Air Force as first operations officer at headquarters and then as bomb-group commander. He led his group on the first American B-17 strike of the war against the Axis (Rouen, France, on 17 August 1942), and in January 1943 he led his group again on the first American mission against a target inside Germany. These experiences led to his portrayal as the fictional General Savage. After tours stateside, Armstrong returned to combat as a B-29 wing commander in the Pacific. Following the war, he taught at the Armed Forces Staff College and commanded a base, an air division, and a numbered air force. In 1956 he pinned on his third star to take over Alaskan Command. Believing that his command was being shortchanged in defense matters, he angrily retired in 1961.

Armstrong wrote two memoirs. The first, "So Near Heaven, Surrounded by Hell," a diary recounting his experiences in Eighth Air Force, is a bit breathless and exuberant, but his intent is to memorialize the brave bomber crews who fought over Germany against heavy odds. His description of the mission over Wilhelmshaven in 1943—the first for the B-17s against a target in Germany—is especially interesting.

After retirement, Armstrong wrote his life story "Awake the Sleeping Giant." Like his first effort, it remains unpublished, and both manuscripts are located in the library of East Carolina University in Greenville, North Carolina. (Copies of "So Near Heaven" are located in the archives at Maxwell AFB, Alabama, and the Air Force Academy.)

Probably the most accomplished intelligence officer in Air Force history, **Charles P. Cabell** graduated from West Point in 1925, flew observation and fighter aircraft for the next decade, and became well known as a photoreconnaissance expert. During the London blitz, he went to Britain to study RAF photointerpretation procedures, and his subsequent report greatly impressed his superiors. As a result, Hap Arnold formed an "advisory council" in early 1942 that initially consisted of only two people, Lauris Norstad and Cabell. Their task was to perform "blue sky thinking" and handle any special projects Arnold threw their way. Often referred to as the "brain trust," the council played an important role in Arnold's somewhat anarchic management style. In 1943 Cabell went to England to command a bomb wing and thence to the Mediterranean to serve as Eaker's chief of intelligence. During the last year of the war, he had fairly extensive dealings with the Soviets over events in the Balkans and soon acquired a healthy respect for and distrust of them. After the war, he served briefly on the US delegation to the United Nations (UN) discussions in London and then returned to the United States in 1948 to become the deputy chief of staff for intelligence for the Air Force as a major general. After two years, he became the director of the joint staff as a three-star, and in 1953 he became the deputy director of the CIA. He remained in that position as a full general until his retirement in 1962.

Cabell wrote a very detailed and interesting autobiography titled "Memoirs of an Unidentified Aide," held by the Air Force Historical Research Agency (AFHRA) at Maxwell AFB, Alabama (although one must obtain permission from his family to quote from the manuscript). Throughout, Cabell takes pains to describe the people with whom he serves, providing excellent personality sketches of such men as Arthur Tedder, Trafford Leigh-Mallory, George Patton, Carl Spaatz, and Ira Eaker. Also of interest is his discussion of the oil campaign conducted by the strategic air forces in 1944–45. This issue caused a great deal of controversy then and has continued to do so. Cabell's treatment is insightful, as is his explanation of the need for a special type of air intelligence that differed fundamentally from the intelligence traditionally required by surface forces. One needed a new organization to gather, analyze, and disseminate this new type of air intelligence; Cabell was instrumental in performing that role. Overall, "Memoirs of an Unidentified Aide" is an excellent study that deserves to be published.

**Nathan F. Twining** succeeded Vandenberg as Air Force chief and then became chairman of the JCS, the first airman to hold that position. Twining came from a rich military background; his forebears had served in the American Army and Navy since the French and Indian War. Twining entered the military for service in World War I but soon received an appointment to West Point. Because the program was shortened so as to produce more officers for combat, he spent only two years at the academy. After graduating in 1919 and serving in the infantry for three years, he transferred to the Air Service. Over the next 15 years, he flew fighter aircraft in Texas, Louisiana, and Hawaii while attending ACTS and Command and General Staff College. When war broke out in Europe, he went to the Operations Division on the Air Staff; then in 1942, he was sent to the South Pacific, where he became chief of staff of the Allied air forces in that area. In January 1943, he assumed command of Thirteenth Air Force, and that November he traveled across the world to take over Fifteenth Air Force from Jimmy Doolittle. When Germany surrendered, Arnold sent Twining back to the Pacific to command the B-29s of Twentieth Air Force in the last push against Japan, but he was there only a short time when the atomic strikes ended the war. He returned to the States and became commander of Air Materiel Command, and in 1947 he took over Alaskan Command. After three years there, he was set to retire as a lieutenant general, but when Muir Fairchild, the vice chief of staff, died unexpectedly of a heart attack, Twining was elevated to full general and named his successor. When Vandenberg retired in mid-1953, Twining became chief; during his tenure, massive retaliation based on airpower became the national strategy. In 1957 President Eisenhower appointed Twining chairman of the joint chiefs.

Surprisingly, the only biography of this famous airman is a dissertation that covers his career up to 1953: J. Britt McCarley's "General Nathan Farragut Twining: The Making of a Disciple of American Strategic Air Power, 1897–1953" (Temple University, 1989). Based largely on secondary sources, official histories, and interviews Twining gave many years after his retirement, McCarley's account provides little insight into Twining's personality, leadership, reasons for success, or his impact on the great events happening around him. In short, the man is lost in the description of events, and by the end of this study, we know little more about Twining than if we had read his entry in *Who's Who*. It is not clear, for example, why Twining was chosen as vice chief of staff in 1953; after all, his performance in the five years after World War II was not impressive. Twining admitted he did not understand why he became commander of Air Materiel Command, and at the time, people considered Alaskan Command a backwater. In fact, McCarley states that the main attraction of this assignment was that it entailed "normal work hours" and allowed Twining plenty of time for hunting and fishing. There is a story here, and McCarley's argument that Twining was chosen because LeMay was unacceptable is inadequate. In addition, McCarley insists on referring to American air doctrine from the 1930s on as "Douhetian." Overall, this dissertation is a poor effort; the important story of Nate Twining still needs telling.

One of the icons of American military history, **Curtis E. LeMay** rivals Mitchell in his importance and controversial career. From middling origins, LeMay did not attend West Point, earning his commission through the Reserve Officer Training Corps (ROTC) in 1928. Over the next decade, he became widely known as one of the best navigators and pilots in the Air Corps. In 1937 he located the battleship *Utah* in exercises off California and "bombed" it with water bombs, despite receiving the wrong coordinates from Navy personnel; the following year, he navigated B-17s nearly 800 miles over the Atlantic Ocean to intercept the Italian liner *Rex* to illustrate airpower's ability to defend the American coasts; and in 1938 he led flights of B-17s to South America to display airpower's range and its role in hemispheric defense.

War brought rapid promotion and increased responsibility. LeMay began as a group commander in Eighth Air Force, but within 18 months he had progressed from lieutenant colonel to major general and had become an air-division commander. He had earned a reputation as an unusually innovative tactician and problem solver, so when Hap Arnold had difficulty bringing the new B-29 into combat service, he chose LeMay to spur the program and then take over B-29 operations in China. LeMay's ability led Arnold to name him commander of the B-29s in the Mariana Islands, where the Allies had concentrated their main air effort against Japan. Always a tactical innovator, LeMay took the risky and controversial step of abandoning the long-held American doctrine of high-altitude, daylight precision bombing; instead, he stripped his B-29s of guns, loaded them with incendiaries, and sent them against Japanese cities at night and at low level. The new strategy proved remarkably successful; Japan was devastated, and the dropping of the atomic bombs in August 1945 brought the Pacific war to an end without an invasion of the Japanese home islands, avoiding the hundreds of thousands of casualties that action would have entailed.

Returning to the States, LeMay served briefly as the head of the AAF's R&D effort and then went to Germany as commander of the air forces in Europe arrayed against the Soviets. In this position, he was responsible for getting the Berlin airlift started in mid-1948, after the Soviets had instituted a ground blockade of the city. This crisis precipitated a major reshuffling in Washington. A war with the Soviets appeared increasingly possible, and many people considered SAC, which would bear the brunt of such a war, deficient. Consequently, Vandenberg relieved Kenney as commander of SAC and named

LeMay his successor. Building SAC into an effective and efficient war-fighting arm was LeMay's greatest accomplishment. One remembers the well-known story of how he demonstrated his command's poor state of readiness by a "bombing raid" on Dayton, Ohio, in which not a single SAC aircraft carried out the mission as planned. He then set about the difficult but essential task of retraining SAC. Using the authority delegated him by Vandenberg, LeMay built new bases, facilities, and training programs; began a "spot promotion" system for rewarding his best aircrews; and, through his legendary use of iron discipline, soon transformed his command into one of the most effective military units in the world.

In 1957 LeMay became vice chief of staff, and when Thomas White retired in 1961, he became chief. Partly because LeMay was one of the coldest of America's cold warriors, his tenure as chief was neither successful nor happy. Under the new management policies of Defense Secretary Robert McNamara and the "flexible response" military strategy of JCS chairman Gen Maxwell D. Taylor, LeMay found himself constantly at odds. In his four years as chief, LeMay argued strenuously for new air weapons like the Skybolt missile and B-70 bomber and against the swing-wing "fighter" plane—the General Dynamics TFX (later named the F-111). He lost all these battles. Moreover, LeMay had strong feelings regarding American involvement in Vietnam, arguing against the gradual response advocated by the administration. Once again he was ignored. When he retired in 1965, LeMay was widely regarded—probably rightly so—as a great commander of SAC but as a poor chief. His abortive political "career" as George Wallace's running mate in the 1968 presidential election only further tarnished the reputation he had built as a war commander and leader of SAC.

LeMay's only biographer to date is Thomas M. Coffey. Like his work on Arnold, discussed above, *Iron Eagle: The Turbulent Life of General Curtis LeMay* (New York: Crown Publishers, 1986) relies too heavily on interviews, newspaper reports, and published memoirs. The book succeeds as an entertaining account of a great man's life and career, but it provides little detail or serious analysis. Coffey is at his best in describing

LeMay's personality: unsophisticated, taciturn, dedicated, tactless to the point of rudeness, more ambitious than he cared to admit, extremely hard working, and possessed of unquestioned physical courage. In addition, Coffey shows that LeMay was also a good family man and sincerely concerned (*sensitive* would be too strong a term) about the welfare of his troops (although the author implies that LeMay's concern stemmed more from his belief that happy subordinates were productive subordinates rather than from any feeling of innate humanitarianism).

This book fails, however, to reveal details surrounding the events in which LeMay participated. His decision to reverse three decades of American airpower doctrine with incendiary attacks against Japanese cities raises profound questions of morality and legality. Coffey simply restates LeMay's rationale that all war is awful and that killing Japanese was better than having them kill Americans. There is something to be said for that point of view, but it is entirely too facile. Are there no limits whatever in warfare? Coffey would seem to imply that none exist. More seriously, the book fails to discuss LeMay's role in the military strategy—or nonstrategy—of the Vietnam War. Unquestionably, the fact that many of his sources remained classified presented a problem, but other than arguing that LeMay never said he wanted to "bomb Vietnam back into the Stone Age," Coffey does not take on this crucial but thorny subject. Later, LeMay stated vehemently that he disagreed with administration policy during the war, but Coffey provides no details about an alternative. Precisely how would LeMay have fought the war? What targets did he intend to strike with airpower, and what effect did he expect those strikes to have? Did he think the Vietcong insurgency in the south would collapse if the leaders in the north were coerced into withdrawing their support? These fundamental questions regarding the role of airpower in a "minor" war have great importance—but they remain unexplored.

Similarly, Coffey identifies the doctrine LeMay advocated as the epitome of strategic bombing, but, once again, he does not examine the implications of such a statement. The book affords no insights into LeMay's theories of warfare and the role of airpower in modern war other than his belief that strategic bombing—lots of it—would be decisive. Was LeMay's thinking truly that simplistic? Perhaps so, because it is unquestionably the case that tactical airpower dangerously atrophied during LeMay's tenure and that the Air Force as a whole became seriously unbalanced. One could argue that because of this overemphasis on SAC, the Air Force found itself woefully unprepared for Vietnam. In light of the subsequent discrediting of airpower, one could legitimately ask whether LeMay actually hurt the cause of American airpower.

One of the more interesting and potentially significant issues that Coffey touches upon is LeMay's strained relations with both Defense Secretary McNamara and Air Force Secretary Eugene Zuckert. Clearly, LeMay believed that these men undermined his prerogatives as chief and military adviser. In fact, McNamara's tenure at Defense serves as a watershed in American military history. Prior to that time, military leaders had some latitude in discussing military affairs with Congress and, to some extent, the public. McNamara saw such a tradition as chaotic and moved to change it by placing constraints on what the chiefs could say and to whom. This is an important story, and although Coffey introduces it, he does not seem to realize its implications. Overall, *Iron Eagle* is a useful read, but we need a more serious study of one of America's most important airmen.

Novelist MacKinlay Kantor assisted LeMay with his autobiography, *Mission with LeMay: My Story* (Garden City, N.Y.: Doubleday, 1965), which is engaging and well written. LeMay's abrupt, no-nonsense personality comes through clearly, and the book provides excellent insight into air leadership. LeMay had intelligence and physical courage—two qualities generally cited as crucial for successful leadership—but his sustained, outstanding performance grew out of his insistence on following a job through until its completion. He relentlessly emphasized rigorous training, and it was this dogged and selfless determination to practice and work hard that made his success possible. One certainly finds a lesson here: great commanders are often made and not born.

**Edwin W. Rawlings** in some ways exemplifies the new Air Force generals who emerged after World War II. Although he had been an observation pilot before the war, he went to Harvard Business School to learn the latest techniques regarding supply and inventory control. As a result, he never secured a combat assignment, which limited his experience during the war to materiel and supply. After the war, he became the first comptroller of the Air Force and in that capacity was instrumental in introducing the first computers into the service. He finished his career in 1959 as a full general and commander of Air Materiel Command. His privately printed autobiography, *Born to Fly* (Minneapolis, Minn.: Great Way Publishing, 1987), recounts these events but is a disappointment. Quite simply, the fact that Rawlings waited too long to write his story clouded his memory of the great events of his career. Instead, we have a series of anecdotes loosely strung together between a discussion of various fishing trips that convey little point or purpose.

Like Rodney Dangerfield, military airlift never gets any respect. Yet, cargo planes and their crews are often the first to respond in a crisis. From Kenney's use of troop transport in the Southwest Pacific to the "Hump" operation over the Himalayas, the Berlin airlift, the reinforcement of Khe Sanh, the resupply of Israel in 1973, and the dropping of food packages in Bosnia, airlift has been a prime factor in American foreign policy. *Over the Hump* (1964; reprint, Washington, D.C.: Office of Air Force History, 1985), the autobiography of **William H. Tunner,** the father of airlift, stands as an excellent chronicle of this important function of airpower.

Tunner begins by describing how in 1929 he received orders to fly a Fokker trimotor from San Diego to Sacramento. He had never flown that type of plane before, had never seen an operator's manual, had no one to explain the plane's systems or characteristics, had no weather forecasters to brief him on the conditions en route, and had a Texaco road map as his only aeronautical chart. He made the flight without incident, but this cavalier attitude towards flying at the time—so well depicted by this anecdote—had a profound effect on Tunner and his subsequent career. After that experience, he became a systematic, organized, and careful pilot.

During World War II, Tunner served as chief of the Ferrying Division of Air Transport Command, performing so well that in 1944 he was selected to take charge of the Hump airlift over the Himalayas. Although his goal was efficiency, one of his prime concerns was safety: the units he supplied wanted their planes and equipment in one piece and in good working order. The feats performed by the C-46s and C-54s that flew supplies into China are the stuff of legend. After cutting his teeth over the Himalayas, Tunner was the obvious choice to direct the operation of the Berlin airlift in 1948–49. Upon arriving in Germany, he found well-meaning, hard-working, and dedicated individuals who were totally disorganized, knew little or nothing about major airlift operations, and were thus quite ineffective. He immediately brought order to the operation, installing flight schedules, precomputed flight plans, rigid air-traffic-control procedures, centralized weather briefings, statistical analyses to determine bottlenecks and problem areas, and strict guidelines for crews' flying times and rest schedules. The results were dramatic: tonnage rates soared, and accident rates dropped. Tunner repeated such performances during the Korean War, and by the time of his retirement in 1960 as a lieutenant general, he had put the Military Air Transport Service (now Air Mobility Command) on a firm professional footing. One of his basic tenets was the uniqueness of airlift. Efficiency and safety were the keys to success—not risk taking and rugged individualism. Tunner's description of the challenges he faced in these operations and his method of dealing with them is insightful, to the point, and extremely interesting. He clearly demonstrates the often forgotten fact that airlift is a tool of peaceful airpower diplomacy. Despite its omission of any evidence of Tunner's legendary temper, *Over the Hump* is an excellent book.

**George E. Stratemeyer** graduated from West Point in 1915—the "class that stars fell on." Among his illustrious classmates were Dwight Eisenhower and Omar Bradley. Initially detailed to the infantry, he switched to the Air Service soon after and became a pilot. Over the next two decades, he flew a number of different aircraft and served in a variety of capacities worldwide. After graduating from the Army War College in 1939, he went to the Air Staff and a year later became the executive officer to Hap Arnold. After a tour as a training-center commander, Stratemeyer returned to Washington to become Arnold's chief of staff as a major general. In mid-1943, he went to the China-Burma-India theater and soon became commander of all air forces in China as a lieutenant general. After the war, he commanded Air Defense Command, Continental Air Command, and FEAF in Tokyo when the Korean War erupted in June 1950. Stratemeyer remained commander through the hectic first year of the war that saw a UN defeat, counterattack and victory, Chinese intervention, a second retreat, and then stabilization of the front. The month following the relief of MacArthur, Stratemeyer suffered a severe heart attack and retired soon thereafter.

Stratemeyer's diary, *The Three Wars of Lt. Gen. George E. Stratemeyer: His Korean War Diary,* ed. William T. Y'Blood (Washington, D.C.: Air Force History and Museums Program, 1999), begun at the start of the Korean War, is a fine effort that includes not only Stratemeyer's diary entries but also copies of numerous messages sent and received by him at the time. Y'Blood has included overviews of historical events then unfolding as well as detailed annotations throughout. The result is a very useful and insightful look at the war from the perspective of the senior airman in-theater.

Like everyone else, Stratemeyer and his command were caught by surprise on 25 June but soon recovered. He quickly realized, however, that his position only partly dealt with leading air forces in war. The book's title speaks to the situation: Stratemeyer felt that he not only had to fight the North Koreans and Chinese but that he also had to engage in a constant, running firefight with the other services and the media. His relations with the other services consumed an enormous amount of time, and his diary is replete with accounts of run-ins with colleagues in different uniforms. These rivalries leaked into the press, precipitating his attempts to shape the reporting of air operations in the war. He seldom passed up an opportunity to solicit tributes from ground commanders regarding the performance of his forces, which he then passed on to the media. Besides the major controversies with the other services over close air support and $C^2$ of air assets, *The Three Wars* also covers the possible use of nuclear weapons, relations with the Nationalist Chinese, intelligence operations, and technical experiments with precision-guided munitions (PGM) and aerial refueling.

Emerging from these pages is a picture of a competent though not dazzling commander. (His main subordinate, Maj Gen Earle "Pat" Partridge, commander of Fifth Air Force, comes across much better.) One cannot help thinking that Stratemeyer, sitting in his air-conditioned office in Tokyo, was somewhat removed from the war—too many entries detail his dinner engagements with noted visitors and golf outings. Additionally, Stratemeyer remained a devoted and loyal follower of MacArthur, often noting what a "great and brilliant man" he was. Just as MacArthur's fortunes waxed and waned, so did Stratemeyer's reflections become more strident. In November 1950, he actually submitted a recommendation for an oak-leaf cluster to MacArthur's Medal of Honor simply because MacArthur was a great American and because he flew a number of reconnaissance missions over Korea in unarmed aircraft. Similarly, when MacArthur commented to him that his superior, Defense Secretary George Marshall, was "an old man" who has "gone nuts," Stratemeyer seems to have concurred. Not surprisingly, Stratemeyer was shocked and dismayed at MacArthur's relief. Six weeks later, he suffered a severe heart attack on a golf course and returned to the States. *The Three Wars* is an important, nicely packaged source for all readers interested not only in the Korean War but also in key, related issues such as interservice rivalry and civil-military affairs.

**Lauris Norstad,** one of the most important and powerful airmen in American history, capped his career as supreme allied commander Europe (SACEUR) from 1956 to 1962. A diplomat as well as a military commander, he was the paradigmatic diplomat-warrior of the modern era.

"Larry" Norstad graduated from West Point in 1930, joined the Air Corps, and for the next decade served as a bomber pilot and staff officer. Despite his youth, he caught Hap Arnold's attention and was one of his principal staff officers throughout World War II. In addition, Norstad flew combat in North Africa, became operations chief for Mediterranean Allied Air Forces, and was chief of staff of Twentieth Air Force during the strategic-bombing campaign against Japan. After the war, Norstad saw duty on the Air Staff in Washington, commanded United States Air Forces Europe, and in 1956 became SACEUR.

At this time, the height of the Cold War, our national strategy called for massive retaliation with nuclear weapons delivered by air. As tactical nuclear weapons and ballistic missiles became available, a major controversy arose within the North Atlantic Treaty Organization (NATO) as to where in the theater the Alliance should deploy these weapons and who should control them.

The British had their own nuclear weapons as well as a "special relationship" with the United States; France aspired to nuclear status and resented US and British primacy within NATO; and West Germany, the obvious battleground if war did break out, was ever fearful of NATO's commitment to West

German security. Norstad had the task of assuaging French pride, maintaining British allegiance, reassuring the Germans, and avoiding any provocation of the Soviets—all the while deterring them from aggressive action. He fulfilled these varied tasks with skill and delicacy.

Robert S. Jordan, a prolific author and NATO expert, tells Norstad's story with unusual insight in *Norstad: Cold War NATO Supreme Commander: Airman, Strategist, Diplomat* (New York: St. Martin's Press, 2000). The highlight of Norstad's tenure as SACEUR, and the event that occupies one-third of the book, is the reemergence of the Berlin crisis. West Berlin, an island in the middle of Soviet-occupied East Germany, was a lightning rod for tension throughout the Cold War. In 1948 the Soviets had blockaded land routes into the city, resulting in the highly successful Berlin airlift, which saved the city from Soviet domination. Beginning in late 1958, the Soviets pressured Berlin once again. The crisis ebbed and flowed over the next four years, culminating in the building of the Berlin Wall. NATO experienced intense strains during that time. The reader may feel a bit overwhelmed by Jordan's detailed account of the crisis, but this is actually a wonderful case study illustrating the enormous complexity that a theater commander must often face in both the military and diplomatic spheres.

Therein lay a problem. The military had heavily involved itself in American politics since the beginning of the Republic, and this involvement intensified after World War II, when numerous military officers served as members of the Cabinet, as ambassadors, and, of course, as president. During his long tenure as SACEUR, Norstad was expected to be a politician as well as an airman. He not only worked with his military counterparts but also dealt frequently and routinely with prime ministers, presidents, and foreign secretaries as well. Troubled by the power and influence Norstad wielded in NATO, President Kennedy and Secretary of Defense McNamara decided to do something about it.

The proximate cause of the rift between Norstad and the Kennedy administration was the issue of flexible response. Although Norstad had long advocated an increase in NATO's conventional strength, he thought Kennedy's calls for a major conventional buildup in Europe were excessive. Throughout the Cold War, some NATO allies felt uneasy over the depth of America's commitment to European defense. To them, a massive conventional buildup served as a signal of the unwillingness of the United States to continue providing a nuclear shield to Europe. According to this view, for deterrence to succeed, one could never allow the Soviets to doubt that the United States would respond to an attack on NATO with *nuclear,* not conventional, weapons. Norstad also disagreed with Kennedy's calculated strategy of gradual escalation during the Berlin crisis. Along with Konrad Adenauer in West Germany, Norstad thought this approach "lacked firmness" and sent the wrong signal to the Soviets. He undoubtedly felt some vindication when the policy of gradual escalation failed so miserably in Vietnam in the years that followed.

Truthfully, the real problem was that Norstad considered himself an international commander first and an American general second. He believed it his duty to pass on the American president's views to NATO and serve as an honest broker in any negotiations that followed. To him, it was not appropriate to follow the orders of a single NATO country—even his own. This belief did not sit well with either Kennedy or McNamara. They wanted a more pliant and less politically visible SACEUR, so in 1962 they nudged Norstad into retirement.

Jordan's book is a first-rate piece of scholarship that contains compelling insights and lessons. Today, one hears much talk that the American military has become politicized and that military involvement in politics runs contrary to American tradition. Although even a cursory review of US history would cast doubt on that contention, our political leaders unquestionably have grown increasingly uneasy with senior military officers straying into the political arena. Norstad was one of the first to fall because of these new concerns. Jordan has done an outstanding job not only of telling the story of an important airman but also of identifying a key milestone in the history of American civil-military affairs.

Because Colin Powell has served as the top military officer in the country and is now secretary of state, some younger Americans have difficulty understanding that the nation's black citizens have not always enjoyed such opportunities. At one point, only a few decades ago, the armed forces remained segregated. Although blacks served, they did so in specialized units—generally commanded by whites—and suffered discrimination not only in promotions but also in fundamental human rights. We have come a long way, but it is useful to recall when such equality did not exist and when racial discrimination was both pervasive and humiliating. During World War II, a group of blacks went to Tuskegee Institute in Alabama to train as pilots. The famous Tuskegee airmen went on to serve with distinction in the European theater and in the nation's military for years thereafter. The most notable of these men was **Benjamin O. Davis Jr.**

The first black to graduate from West Point in the twentieth century, Davis did not have a pleasant four years there. Because of his race, he was officially "silenced" by all cadets—no one spoke to him during his entire stay except on official business; he roomed alone; and he had no friends. That so many cadets, faculty members, and senior officers could allow such behavior is astonishing and surely stands as one of the most shameful chapters in West Point history. Nevertheless, Davis graduated but was promptly turned down for pilot training—no black officers were allowed in the Air Corps. While he served in the infantry in 1940, however, the service reconsidered this policy, and Davis went to Tuskegee for pilot training. Because of the war and his ability, promotion followed rapidly, and he soon found himself a lieutenant colonel commanding the 99th Fighter Squadron in combat. After one year with this all-black unit in Italy, Davis was promoted to colonel and tasked to form the 322d Group, a black fighter unit that served admirably for the remainder of the war.

After a presidential decree ended segregation in the services in 1948, Davis attended Air War College, served in the Pentagon, and went to Korea in 1953 to command a fighter wing. The following year, he received his first star and moved to the Philippines as vice commander of Thirteenth Air Force at Clark Air Base (AB). After tours in Taiwan, Germany, the Pentagon, and a return to Korea—gaining two more stars in the process—Davis became commander of the Thirteenth. Obviously relishing this command at the height of the Vietnam War, he was reluctant to leave in July 1968 to become deputy commander of US Strike Command. He retired from that assignment in 1970.

Surprisingly, no one has written a biography of the first black Air Force general. For now, however, we must content ourselves with his autobiography, *Benjamin O. Davis, Jr., American: An Autobiography* (Washington, D.C.: Smithsonian Institution Press, 1991), an extremely well written memoir. Some reviewers have commented that Davis was obsessed by his West Point experience; although that is too strong a statement, clearly he was deeply affected by it. (Actually, most cadets are deeply affected by their academy experience, but few have such negative memories as did Davis.) The humiliation he suffered there stayed with him his entire career, and not until 1987—more than 50 years after his graduation—did he return for a visit. This book is marked throughout by a sense of patriotism and faith—especially in himself and his cadet sweetheart, who became his wife and supported him unfalteringly throughout his career. In one sense, this is a moving and touching love story. One may, however, criticize *Benjamin O. Davis, Jr., American* for its insufficient discussion of the key operational issues Davis faced in his several commands in three different wars. The issue of race overshadows everything and takes priority in his recollection of events. As a consequence, we are left with a poignant story that reveals clearly why Benjamin Davis became a successful man but not why he became an equally successful senior commander.

Another of the great Tuskegee airmen, **Daniel "Chappie" James Jr.,** won his wings and a commission in 1943 but did not see combat in World War II. After the war, James quickly earned a reputation as an outstanding fighter pilot. In Korea he flew 100 combat missions, and in Vietnam—by 1965 he was a full colonel—he flew over threescore more. Not only was that war unpopular but also racial unrest was exploding into violence all over the United States at the time. Returning from Vietnam, James was often called upon to defend America's racial policies as well as its military policies. An articulate speaker with great physical presence (he was six feet, four inches tall and weighed nearly 250 pounds), he was an especially effective spokesman for the Air Force. In 1967 he became commander of Wheelus AB in Libya just as Mu'ammar Gadhafi succeeded in his revolution there. Gadhafi demanded that the air base—which he saw as a vestige of European colonialism—be closed and its facilities turned over to the Libyan people. This obviously was an extremely delicate position for James, requiring restraint, tact, diplomacy, and grit, which he displayed in abundance. Upon leaving Wheelus a year later, he received his first star. After four years in the Pentagon working in Public Affairs, where he won two more stars, he became vice commander of Military Airlift Command (MAC). After less than two years at MAC, he received a fourth star—the first black in American history to attain that rank—and assumed command of NORAD. For a man of his size and appearance, James was in surprisingly poor health. After suffering a heart attack in 1977, he elected to retire soon thereafter. His health continued to decline, and in February 1978, one month after retirement, he suffered a fatal heart attack.

In one of the two biographies of the general, James R. McGovern's *Black Eagle, General Daniel "Chappie" James, Jr.* (University, Ala.: University of Alabama Press, 1985), the author portrays James as a patriotic, hard-working, articulate, and measured individual who served as a convincing spokesman for the black cause without becoming radicalized. James constantly stressed the qualities of determination and sincerity, arguing that people should be judged by their performance, not skin color. McGovern takes a balanced approach. He notes the rumors that James avoided combat in Vietnam and that his rapid rise in rank was politically motivated, but also points to his abilities as a more-than-capable commander and his outstanding performance in the difficult Libyan situation. Clearly, James deserved his promotion to flag rank. Less satisfactory is McGovern's explanation of James's advancement from that point on. Granted, he was an effective and dynamic speaker who performed his duties in public affairs in an exemplary fashion, but those duties do not in themselves justify promotion to lieutenant general. Moreover, the decision to give James his fourth star—usually, only about 12 full generals serve in the Air Force at a given time—rested on his performance as vice commander of MAC. But McGovern dismisses this two-year assignment with a single sentence. Also, the book devotes barely one page to James's three-year tenure as NORAD commander. As a result, although readers have a clear portrait of James's role as a civil-rights pioneer, they do not acquire an understanding of his performance as a senior commander.

The other biography of James, J. Alfred Phelps's *Chappie: America's First Black Four-Star General: The Life and Times of Daniel James, Jr.* (Novato, Calif.: Presidio Press, 1991), is even less satisfactory. Phelps uses James as a symbol of integration, showing how blacks rose from their inferior status in World War II to acceptance three decades later. Unfortunately, this portrayal is marred by a tone both too strident and too glowing. For example, the author devotes several chapters to the racial problems faced by the Tuskegee airmen during the war but admits that James played almost no role in those events. Like the McGovern work, from which Phelps borrows heavily, this book's explanation of James's mercurial rise in rank after 1969 remains inadequate. Phelps asserts rather than demonstrates the general's competence and relies far too heavily on public-relations speeches by James to illustrate his points. As a result, both of these biographies leave readers with more questions than answers.

 **Edward G. Lansdale,** one of the most unusual senior Air Force leaders, originally served as an Army intelligence officer and an agent for the Office of Strategic Services in World War II, transferring to the Air Force when it became a separate service in 1947. At the same time, he joined the CIA and for the next two decades pursued dual careers. CIA director William Colby later called Lansdale one of the 10 greatest spies of all time.

Because Lansdale had closely studied the theories of revolutionary warfare espoused by Mao Tse-tung—undertaken during his stay at the Pentagon between 1948 and 1950—he was posted to the Philippines in late 1950, at the height of the communist-backed Huk rebellion. Lansdale soon became close friends with Philippine defense minister Ramón Magsaysay. The two men exchanged ideas and worked closely together on a plan to eradicate the Huk menace. In essence, both realized that attempts to deal with the rebellion up to that time had involved solely military forces. Yet, the concerns of average Filipinos that made them susceptible to Huk propaganda were largely economic and political in nature. The solutions, therefore, had to be economic and political as well. A measure of the veracity of this insight—so radical at the time— is its acceptance today as conventional wisdom in counterinsurgency strategy.

Lansdale was largely responsible for developing a robust psychological-warfare campaign to win back the hearts of the Filipino people. The election of Magsaysay as president in November 1953 ensured the swift and effective implementation of these ideas, resulting in the rapid elimination of the Huks as a threat—militarily, politically, and psychologically.

In January 1954, Lansdale, now a colonel, arrived in South Vietnam as a "special adviser" as well as CIA station chief. There, he attempted to replicate his success in the Philippines, becoming a close adviser to Ngo Dinh Diem, whom he saw on almost a daily basis over the next three years, and laboring to nudge him towards a broader-based and more open form of government. This difficult task was exacerbated by the sizable French military presence in the south, which bitterly opposed not only Diem but also the upstart Americans. Moreover, Lansdale found himself frequently at odds with his own government, which was little disposed towards Diem. Nevertheless, the south made progress against the communist insurgents, and when Lansdale left Vietnam in 1956, he had reason for optimism—which would prove unfounded. After several years in the Pentagon as special assistant to the secretary of defense in the area of special operations, he retired in 1963 as a major general.

As events worsened in Vietnam, Lansdale was asked to return in 1965, in mufti, as a special assistant to Ambassador Henry Cabot Lodge. This tour, largely a failure, proved enormously frustrating for him. His ideas ran contrary to those of Lodge, as well as those of Gen William C. Westmoreland. Like virtually everyone else, the Tet offensive of February 1968 caught Lansdale by surprise. He resigned soon after and retired again to Virginia. A unique individual widely known for his dual role as military officer and spy, he became the model for main characters in two best-selling novels: *The Ugly American* and *The Quiet American* (in the former, his character went by the unlikely name of Ed Hillandale). In a sense, he symbolized all the best and worst of American involvement in Southeast Asia.

Several things call attention to themselves in Lansdale's very personal, interesting, and provocative memoir *In the Midst of Wars: An American's Mission to Southeast Asia* (New York: Harper & Row, 1972), which focuses exclusively on his years in the Philippines, 1950–53, and in South Vietnam, 1954–57. First, he believed deeply that protracted revolutionary wars were not inevitably destined for success—a contrary opinion at the time. Such rebellions represented a new form of war that governments were unprepared to deal with effectively; once they understood the nature of such wars, however, they could produce counterstrategies. The key to success against insurgents lay in using political action to win the support of the people. That achieved, the insurgency would wither and die. Lansdale also stressed the need for American advisers to truly understand the needs and desires of the common people by getting out into the countryside and avoiding the bureaucracy of the capital city. He followed his own advice almost too well, barely evading ambushes and assassination attempts on numerous occasions. Nevertheless, these personal insights were essential to a successful counterinsurgency because, in Lansdale's view, "Washington" almost never understands the true state of affairs.

Clearly, Lansdale had some axes to grind. His depiction of the French in Vietnam is uniformly bad: they come across as haughty, corrupt, spiteful, and duplicitous, whereas Diem is portrayed as an honest, hardworking, and courageous patriot who simply did not have adequate support from the US government—an unusual interpretation. This account suffers from two glaring omissions. First, Lansdale never mentions his status as a CIA agent; second, he does not discuss his return to Vietnam in the mid-1960s, which ended so unhappily. No doubt, security considerations contributed to these oversights, but one cannot help feeling that Lansdale is simply indulging in another of the innumerable "disinformation campaigns" at which he proved so adept.

One finds a more detailed and completer portrait of this unusual figure in Cecil B. Currey's *Edward Lansdale, The Unquiet American* (Boston: Houghton Mifflin, 1988). In one sense, Currey's timing was ideal: Lansdale, alive and candid, had achieved a sense of perspective concerning the events he helped shape, and he willingly revealed to his biographer some of his secret activities. Clearly, Currey established excellent rapport with his subject; unfortunately, Lansdale died while Currey's manuscript was in draft. Although the author relies far too heavily on Lansdale's account of events, we still have a fairly balanced chronicle of a man who, in some ways, was a near genius in his ability to understand Asian cultures and see to the core of complex problems. On the other hand, Lansdale's opinions, aggressiveness, and petulance earned him numerous enemies throughout the US military and government, as well as among foreign militaries and governments. Overall, Lansdale's extraordinary abilities come through in this biography, but at the same time, Currey deftly paints a highly critical portrait of America's (and Lansdale's) unsubtle efforts to manipulate and bribe foreign officials and shape their policies—activities that eventually created far more problems than they solved.

One of the young pilots sent to Europe in World War II who quickly rose to high rank because the life expectancy of combat aircrews was so brief, **George S. Brown** graduated from West Point in 1941 and only three years later became a full colonel. On one of his most famous missions, he led a bomb group over Ploesti, winning a Distinguished Service Cross for his efforts. The downside was that it took him an additional 15 years to receive his next promotion. In those intervening years, Brown served as commander of bomber, transport, and fighter units; as assistant operations officer of FEAF during the Korean War; and as executive officer for Thomas White, the Air Force chief of staff. After two years in this last position, Brown received his first star and became military assistant to Secretary of Defense McNamara. After leaving the Pentagon in 1963 as a major general, Brown became commander of Twentieth Air Force (airlift) for two years and then returned to the Pentagon as special assistant to the chairman of the JCS (Gen Earle Wheeler). Promoted to full general, he went to Vietnam in 1968 to command Seventh Air Force. Interestingly, as Brown left for Vietnam, John Ryan, then the Air Force chief of staff, told him he was being groomed to take over as chief a few years hence. As a result, when Brown returned to the States in 1970, he was named commander of Air Force Systems Command, "to make him well rounded." As promised, when Ryan retired in 1972, Brown became chief. After less than nine months in that position, however, Brown was elevated to JCS chairman, the first airman to hold that position since Nate Twining 15 years earlier. During his tenure as chairman, Vietnam, Laos, and Cambodia fell; SALT II was negotiated; Cyprus erupted; US marines stormed the *Mayaguez;* and North Koreans hacked an Army officer to death. In addition, Brown found himself in hot water on two occasions when he gave speeches interpreted as "anti-Israel." Although some people called for his immediate dismissal, the chairman survived these incidents. Unfortunately, he did not survive cancer. Like Hoyt Vandenberg two decades before, Brown spent his last months in office in constant pain. He retired in June 1978 and died of cancer six months later.

In the only biography of Brown, Edgar F. Puryear Jr.'s *George S. Brown, General, U.S. Air Force: Destined for Stars* (Novato, Calif.: Presidio Press, 1983), the author concludes that the general's honesty, integrity, sincerity, and intelligence made him successful. More of a character study than a biography, the book relies on scores of interviews that relate what Brown was like, how he interacted with his superiors and subordinates, how he managed his staff meetings, and so forth. However, this focus on George Brown the man and the officer omits the actual environment in which he worked and the problems he had to address. What we have is a seemingly endless stream of anecdotes and testimonials regarding the general's personality—but precious few facts on precisely what he did as a senior leader. For example, Puryear relates how Brown, the assistant operations officer for FEAF during the second year of the Korean War, interacted with his colleagues and what they thought of him—but includes scarcely any discussion of the war. The book also fails to mention issues such as the close air support controversy with the Army and Marines and the definition of "coordination control" with the Navy. The result is a somewhat unsatisfactory character sketch devoid of substance.

Regrettably, only a handful of senior airmen have written memoirs in the past four decades. One of these, **James V. Hartinger's** *From One Stripe to Four Stars* (Colorado Springs, Colo.: Phantom Press, 1997), provides a fairly brief overview of his long career, which began when he was drafted into the Army during World War II. In 1945 he pinned on sergeant's stripes shortly before receiving an appointment to West Point. Graduating in 1949, Hartinger transferred to the Air Force "because you get more money there," earned his wings, and became a fighter pilot. He flew combat tours in Korea and Vietnam, served as a wing commander and an action officer in the Pentagon, became commandant of the Air War College, twice commanded a numbered air force (Ninth and Twelfth), and in 1980 became commander in chief of NORAD soon after receiving his fourth star. Significantly, when Air Force Space Command stood up in 1982, the "dual hatted" Hartinger served as its first head. He retired from those positions in 1984.

Hartinger's is not a traditional memoir in that it provides little insight into most subjects regarding his career. Although each chapter corresponds to a specific assignment, some of them are only a page or two long. Moreover, he completely ignores crucial topics that would ordinarily be de rigueur for such a memoir. For example, although he flew in both Korea and Vietnam, the book scarcely mentions his activities in these wars. In the case of Vietnam, this slight is especially remarkable because Hartinger was chief of Seventh Air Force's command center in Saigon and flew 100 combat missions. In his words, "few people in Vietnam knew more about the conduct of the war than I did." Yet, he never discusses the many things he saw and learned: American goals, the targets selected for air attack and the rationale for their selection, the effectiveness of air strikes, logistics, intelligence operations, interservice cooperation/rivalry, and so forth. Similarly, Hartinger played a pivotal role in the decision to form Space

Command, which has had far-reaching and long-lasting consequences, yet the only justification he provides for this momentous proposal is that "space is like the land, the sea, and the air. It's a theater of operations." Certainly, a great deal more thought went into it than that. Although he served as commandant of Air War College, Hartinger has almost nothing to say about education. What was the mission of the school? What were the students supposed to learn about the application of airpower? How would this education enhance their professionalism and utility to the Air Force? What qualifications did he look for in his faculty members? Indeed, the sole comment he makes on his role as one of the Air Force's chief educators concerns his obvious pleasure in cutting the length of student writing assignments!

Rather, Hartinger has written a book on leadership by demonstrating how individualism, involvement, and energy shaped his own career and how they can shape anyone else's. Beginning with his experiences as a star athlete in high school and college—a member of the Lacrosse Hall of Fame, he was a three-time All American lacrosse player at West Point—he offers many examples of how he practiced the art of leadership. As a consequence, the reader encounters numerous vignettes and morality plays designed to demonstrate how leaders should take care of their troops, build teamwork, accomplish the mission, and offer unpopular advice to superiors. In this respect, *From One Stripe to Four Stars* achieves some success and, therefore, is useful as a leadership primer for cadets and junior officers.

**Charles A. Horner,** an Iowa farm boy who had a hankering to fly, joined the Air Force ROTC unit at the University of Iowa, receiving his commission upon graduation in 1958. A fighter pilot, he flew two tours in Vietnam, and over a 35-year career, he served as commander of a squadron, a wing, an air division, and an air force—and as commander in chief of US Space

Command. He is most remembered, however, for his stint as coalition air commander during the Persian Gulf War in 1991. In that position, Horner presided over one of the most decisive military victories in history, achieved with astonishingly low casualties. With Tom Clancy, he tells his story with unusual candor, clarity, and force in *Every Man a Tiger* (New York: Putnam, 1999).

All too often, such ghosted memories are little more than adventure stories with few insights—but this book is an exception. The Clancy/Horner combination has produced an outstanding effort. Switching back and forth between Clancy's narrative and Horner's "color commentary," we read things that either man alone probably would not have written. For example, who would describe himself, as Clancy does Horner, as having "a comfortable but not pretty, bloodhound face, sandy, thinning hair, and a bulldog body"? Similarly, could Clancy have known that Horner has a strong aversion for people arguing about whether aircraft are "strategic" or "tactical"? Horner tells us that only "airheaded airmen" continue to abuse such terms.

Horner provides an excellent description of the frustration and anger that he and so many of his colleagues felt during the Vietnam War. We are all products of our past, and it is plain that Horner was deeply affected by the stupidity, waste, and duplicity he saw in Vietnam. When he got his chance to lead in combat in Operation Desert Storm, he was determined to do things differently. In a frank and self-deprecating fashion, Horner relates his thoughts on the crisis of 1990–91 and his use of airpower. Horner's insights are the best written to date and, given his position, are the best likely to be written.

When Saddam Hussein's forces invaded Kuwait in August 1990, Horner was commander of Ninth Air Force, which meant he also functioned as joint force air component commander for all air assets that would see action in Desert Storm. He sheds fascinating light on the planning and execution of the air campaign. With neither anger nor hubris, he offers character sketches of the key coalition players, discusses the Instant Thunder air campaign plan devised by John Warden, and shares his thoughts on the relief of Gen Mike Dugan, then the Air Force chief of staff. He takes much pride in his account of the war, basking in the professionalism, courage, and ingenuity demonstrated by airmen of all ranks, services, and countries during the greatest aerial success story in history. One must remember that such stunning success was not inevitable. Many ideas put forth during the crisis would have tragically misused the unique advantages of airpower. He singles out Gen Norman Schwarzkopf for having the wisdom to see beyond his experience as a soldier and understand the possibilities of an air campaign. If Schwarzkopf had not had such flexibility of vision, the war could have lasted far longer and been far bloodier.

Horner is especially good at discussing the importance of coalition relationships. Remembering how condescendingly Americans had treated their South Vietnamese allies and the problems such an attitude had caused, he insisted on treating the coalition members as equals. The book makes clear that the duties of a senior coalition commander entail far more than the "mere" planning and executing of a military campaign. Similarly, Horner emphasizes the necessity for jointness. War is too important to compound its risk with foolish interservice rivalries. In this regard, the Marines were a constant disappointment to him, "playing games" throughout the war and seemingly unable to put service parochialism aside, even though lives were at stake.

The other valuable aspect of this memoir is its insight into the employment of airpower. Horner spends much time explaining his thought processes for various decisions, constantly asking himself, "What will the enemy do next; what *could* he do next; how would I respond?" He recounts the air battle at Khafji, Saudi Arabia, where coalition airpower mauled three Iraqi divisions, thus ending any chance of an enemy ground offensive. Horner repeats the key principle that all of us must ever bear in mind: air superiority is always the first and most important priority; without it, all military operations become difficult, if not impossible.

At the same time, Horner admits his mistakes. He grossly underestimated the danger from Scud missiles, failing to devise tactics to effectively halt their use. Furthermore, he permitted low-level operations that resulted in the loss of several coalition aircraft. Horner's concluding thoughts on space and the way it has changed war are also important, although one would like to see this section expanded. Nevertheless, *Every Man a Tiger* is an excellent and enjoyable book—one of the finest memoirs written to date by a high-ranking airman.

Chapter 3

# Anthologies and Oral Histories

Several anthologies contain brief biographies of leading airmen. Edgar F. Puryear Jr. writes about leadership in *Stars in
Flight: A Study in Air Force Character and Leadership* (San
Rafael, Calif.: Presidio Press, 1981), concentrating on the first
five leaders of the modern Air Force: Hap Arnold, Carl Spaatz,
Hoyt Vandenberg, Nate Twining, and Thomas White. He bases
his research largely on his interviews and correspondence
with general officers who knew or worked for these men.
Puryear concludes that one can sum up the key to leadership
in five qualities—duty, honor, service, courage (both moral and
physical), and decisiveness—possessed by his subjects. As
with his biography of George Brown, this book is not successful. Because Puryear's audience consists of cadets or junior
officers, the biographical sketches amount to hero building
rather than critical analysis. In addition, his heavy reliance on
interviews and letters reduces the study to little more than a
series of quotations and stories strung together with little
cohesion or overall point. One does, however, gain some
insight into the personalities of these men—a useful starting
point for someone wanting to undertake a serious study.

In *Fighting Airmen* (New York: Putnam, 1966), Curt Anders
aims to describe the lives of seven great American airmen:
Billy Mitchell, "who had the initial vision"; Curtis LeMay, who
brought that vision "to its closest approximation in practice";
and five others who kept that vision alive through their combat leadership—Eddie Rickenbacker, Hap Arnold, Jimmy
Doolittle, Claire Chennault, and George Kenney. Unfortunately, the book amounts to little more than an unbalanced
series of tributes. As with Puryear's book, however, it contains
some information that would prove useful to someone starting
a serious investigation of air leadership.

David MacIsaac's "Leadership in the Old Air Force: A Post-
graduate Assignment," the Harmon Memorial Lecture for 1987,
in *The Harmon Memorial Lectures in Military History, 1959–1987,*

ed. Harry R. Borowski (Washington, D.C.: Office of Air Force History, 1988), is an extremely well written and unusual piece about the early careers of Hap Arnold, Carl Spaatz, and Ira Eaker.

The best of the anthologies, *Makers of the United States Air Force,* ed. John L. Frisbee (1987; reprint, Washington, D.C.: Air Force History and Museums Program, 1996), contains chapter-length biographical sketches of Benjamin Foulois (by John Shiner), Frank Andrews (by DeWitt Copp), Harold L. George (by Haywood Hansell Jr.), Hugh Knerr (by Murray Green), George Kenney (by Herman Wolk), William E. Kepner (by Paul Henry), Elwood R. Quesada (by John Schlight), Hoyt S. Vandenberg (by Noel Parrish), Benjamin O. Davis Jr. (by Alan Gropman), Nathan F. Twining (by Donald Mrozek), Bernard A. Schriever (by Jacob Neufeld), and Robinson Risner (by T. R. Milton). Frisbee selected these individuals not only because of their importance but also because they had received insufficient attention from historians. Although the essays lack documentation, they are of a high caliber and describe both the personalities of the men and their significance.

The most interesting essays deal with "the forgotten airmen." Frank Andrews, the first commander of GHQ Air Force in 1935 and the first airman ever promoted to three-star rank, served as commander of the European theater at the time of his death in a plane crash in 1943. Hal George, one of the key figures in the development of bombardment doctrine at ACTS in the 1930s, helped author AWPD-1 and served as wartime head of Air Transport Command. A famous balloonist in the interwar years and head of VIII Fighter Command at the time of "Big Week" in February 1944, William Kepner finished the war as commander of Eighth Air Force. Bernard Schriever was a pilot-turned-engineer, now considered the father of the ICBM program. And Robbie Risner, a fighter pilot and ace in the Korean War, won the first-ever Air Force Cross in 1965 over the skies of Vietnam and endured seven years as a prisoner of war in North Vietnam. *Makers of the United States Air Force* is an excellent book and should encourage historians seeking a topic worthy of a full-length biography. All of its subjects are excellent candidates.

Another effort, sponsored and published by the Office of Air Force History in 1986, is *Air Leadership: Proceedings of a Con-*

*ference at Bolling Air Force Base, April 13–14, 1984,* edited by
Wayne Thompson. Several contributions to the book emphasize
differing leadership styles. Papers on two airmen, Carl Spaatz (by
Dave Mets and I. B. Holley) and William Moffett (by Thomas
Hone), were singled out for examination. (Other papers discussed RAF-AAF relations during World War II and the manager-
versus-leader debate in the postwar Air Force.) Although these
biographical sketches are useful, of greater interest are the panel
discussions by luminaries such as Gen Curtis LeMay, Gen Mark
Bradley, Gen Bryce Poe, Gen Brian Gunderson, and Gen Alfred
F. Hurley. The reminiscences of these men, prompted by questions from the audience, are quite enlightening.

DeWitt S. Copp wrote two very popular books that trace the
history of Army aviation from the Wright brothers through World
War II: *A Few Great Captains: The Men and Events That Shaped
the Development of U.S. Air Power* (Garden City, N.Y.: Doubleday,
1980), which ends in 1939, and *Forged in Fire: Strategy and Decisions in the Air War over Europe, 1940–45* (Garden City, N.Y.:
Doubleday, 1982), which covers the war years. Though not biographies, they tell the history of the air arm through the eyes of
various air leaders, especially Hap Arnold, Frank Andrews, Carl
Spaatz, and Ira Eaker. The biggest disappointment for the reader
is that Copp never finished the story—he spends barely 30 pages
on the last two years of the war—and never completed a projected third volume. Consequently, the great airmen who would
dominate both the last two years of war and the postwar era—
Vandenberg, Twining, White, and LeMay—barely receive an
introduction. In addition, despite Copp's prodigious research, he
includes few notes—most of them explanatory—which prevents
readers from taking a closer look at his sources and interpreta-
tions. Finally, his treatment of the icons of American airpower
borders on hagiography; one finds scarcely a discouraging word.
Nevertheless, Copp's very entertaining, mostly accurate books
tell the story of American airpower with passion and verve.

Flint O. DuPre's *U.S. Air Force Biographical Dictionary* (New
York: Franklin Watts, 1965), a reference work that has proven
invaluable to many researchers, contains biographical
sketches of American airmen who achieved at least three-star
rank or who became famous for other reasons (e.g., Medal of

Honor winners, Air Service/Air Corps chiefs, Air Force secretaries, etc.). Sadly, this well-done and important tool is now out of date and in need of a major revision that would add sketches of airmen from the past three decades.

Oral histories can also be of great use to a researcher, despite serious pitfalls peculiar to the genre (e.g., memories of past events are often clouded; people sometimes tell the interviewer what they think he or she wants to hear; few people are willing to admit their biggest or most embarrassing mistakes; and score settling is common fare). Interviews can set a tone for a particular era or event as well as provide valuable context. In addition, interviews often reveal personality traits, quirks, conflicts, and connections not recorded in written histories. For example, it came as a great surprise to me to learn from one transcripted interview that a certain high-ranking individual was an alcoholic. The issue came up in passing—something that had not entered my mind as a possibility but that had significant implications. With this revelation—confirmed in other interviews—other issues, decisions, and actions took on a far different light. The major caveat to consider is that the interview can open doors to interesting rooms, but a thorough examination of those rooms requires more conventional and definitive research methods.

Three organizations in particular have been especially active in interviewing distinguished airmen regarding their careers: the AFHRA at Maxwell AFB, Alabama; the History Department at the Air Force Academy in Colorado Springs; and a group of researchers at Columbia University in New York City. AFHRA's collection is by far the largest of the three, containing over 2,000 interviews. It is also quite broad, covering all periods and subjects. The Air Force Academy, on the other hand, tends to concentrate on specific subjects dealing with the academy's history. For example, interviewers have conducted fascinating sessions with a number of graduates held captive during the Vietnam and Persian Gulf Wars. For abstracts of interviews conducted by the AFHRA and the Air Force Academy, see *Catalog of the United States Air Force Oral History Collection,* ed. Maurice Maryanow (Maxwell AFB, Ala.: AFHRA, 1989). Columbia University's very large collection of oral histories contains only a small number of interviews concerning airpower. For a list of them, see *The Oral History Collection of Columbia University,* 4th ed., ed. Elizabeth B. Mason and Louis M. Starr (New York: Oral History Research Office, 1979).

# Chapter 4

# **Conclusion**

Excluding the thousands of oral histories extant, I have included 93 studies in part one of this book—more than I expected to find when I began this project. Their quality is quite uneven, and one finds other anomalies: too many books on Claire Chennault and too few on Jimmy Doolittle. Despite Doolittle's importance and the six biographies of him, his significance and leadership remain obscure. Although we know enough of the details of Doolittle's life, we still need an analysis of and explanation for his success as the commander of some of our most important air units at particularly crucial times. Similarly, one doubts that new facts about the lives of Billy Mitchell, Hap Arnold, or Curtis LeMay will come to light; yet, works that analyze the impact these men had on the Air Force and its perception by the other services, Congress, and the public would add significantly to the literature.

Amazingly, however, biographers have virtually ignored some truly great airmen. First among them is Nate Twining. Others in need of a biography include John P. McConnell, chief of staff during the early years of the Vietnam War; John D. Ryan, who succeeded McConnell as chief during Vietnam; Muir "Santy" Fairchild, an instructor in the Bombardment Section at ACTS, joint planner during World War II, and vice chief under Vandenberg; Thomas White; Frank Andrews; Larry Kuter; Emmett "Rosie" O'Donnell, who commanded B-29s in World War II and Korea and retired while commander of Pacific Air Forces at the beginning of the Vietnam War; Bernard Schriever; Otto "Opie" Weyland, another great tactical airman who fought in three major wars; Harold L. George; David Jones, chief of staff and chairman of the JCS, who led the fight to reform the military during the first Reagan administration; James Fechet, Air Corps chief between Patrick and Foulois; Benjamin Davis; Jeanne Holm, the first woman to reach flag rank in the Air Force; and William Momyer, perhaps the most creative and innovative of the tactical airmen, who commanded Seventh Air Force in Vietnam and TAC afterwards. Information about airmen who served as engineers or involved themselves in R&D constitutes another gap in the literature. Perhaps a volume that includes the biographies of men like George Brett, Oliver Echols, Benjamin Chidlaw, Laurence Craigie, and Donald Putt, and that discusses the technical evolution of airpower during and after World War II would be appropriate.

In addition, something must be done to encourage senior air leaders to write their memoirs. We desperately need to know their stories. Those whose accounts would be most useful include T. R. "Ross" Milton, bomb leader at Schweinfurt, Germany, chief of staff of the Berlin airlift, chief of staff of NATO, and member of the [Walt] Rostow mission to Vietnam; William Momyer (Momyer did publish a book, *Airpower in Three Wars* [Washington, D.C.: Department of the Air Force, 1978], but it is more a comment on tactical air operations in World War II, Korea, and Vietnam than a memoir); Bernard Schriever; David Jones; Lew Allen, chief of staff and transitional figure between the era dominated by SAC and the one dominated by TAC; Russell Dougherty, commander of SAC and one of the great strategic thinkers in Air Force history; Robin Olds, fighter ace and war hero in two different wars; Brent Scowcroft, national security adviser to President George H. Bush; Larry Welch, chief of staff when the Soviet empire collapsed; and Merrill McPeak, chief of staff during the Gulf War and during the momentous reorganization and downsizing that followed.

Another overlooked but important biographical source is the papers—both official and personal—of senior airmen. Located in the Library of Congress, the papers of Mitchell, Arnold, Spaatz, Vandenberg, Twining, LeMay, Eaker, and others are enormous and detailed, giving vital insights into key events in airpower history. One can find numerous other such collections of papers archived at the AFHRA, the Air Force Academy, various presidential libraries, and other private repositories around the country. It is time someone collected, edited, annotated, and published some of these collections. The papers of Arnold and Spaatz are the two most obvious places to start, not only because of the important roles these men played but also the size and significance of their collections.

Tellingly, the papers of Army leaders like George Marshall, Dwight Eisenhower, George Patton, and Lucius Clay have been published in multivolume sets. These have proven invaluable to researchers and historians who require primary-source materials but cannot spend several weeks on a research trip to Washington, D.C., or, in the case of Eisenhower, Abilene, Kansas. Airpower demands the same availability of such materials. We need editors knowledgeable of airpower history along with agencies willing to lend financial support to such a great effort. The publication of *Selected Works, 1990–1994* (Maxwell AFB, Ala.: Air University Press, 1995), the speeches made by Gen "Tony" McPeak when he was chief of staff, is a welcome addition to the literature; all the chiefs should follow suit.

In sum, although much has been done already, very much more remains to be done. Carl Builder has commented that the Air Force culture is dominated by technology, not people. In one sense, he is correct, but technology is always the tool of men and women, and we must never lose sight of the human element in air warfare. Although biography has its limitations—a tendency to exaggerate the significance of individuals and to forget that institutions, groups, and simple fate can also determine history—the insights into character, culture, behavior, and emotion far outweigh any potential drawbacks. We have much to learn from our past leaders. The challenges they faced are not so different from those we confront today and will meet in the future. Thorough, critical, dispassionate, and honest biographies and autobiographies are essential in assisting future airmen meet their challenges.

# PART 2

## The Historiography of Airpower Theory and Doctrine

# Chapter 5

# **Overall Treatments**

The history of military theory and doctrine is a subset of military history. Theory and doctrine deal with the realm of ideas, not operations, and partly because of this, fewer people have been inclined to write about this more esoteric subject. As a result, tracing the history of ideas has proven to be a fairly barren field. The problem becomes far worse regarding airpower. Airmen, regardless of nationality, have seldom been accused of being thinkers, and precious few have taken up the pen to write down their thoughts on how one should employ airpower in war. Added to this is the relatively short length of time airpower has existed: just in the past century. As a result, only a limited number of books, articles, and manuals that deal with the theory and doctrine of airpower have appeared to date.

The aim of this and the following chapters is to enumerate and assess those works of airpower theory and doctrine and to reveal the historiography of ideas on conventional airpower employment.* The subject of nuclear-deterrence theory and its associated doctrines of mutual assured destruction, strategic sufficiency, and the like are a separate and enormous field that I do not address here. Similarly, I do not discuss space, a field growing in importance and interest. In addition, I admit to a major limitation: I cover only those items written or translated into English. Undoubtedly, many more important works have appeared in French, German, Russian, and other languages. Those I must leave to someone more capable.

Only one book attempts to give a history of airpower theory and trace its evolution during the twentieth century. The compendium produced by the School of Advanced Airpower Studies (SAAS), *The Paths of Heaven: The Evolution of Airpower The-*

---

*A version of Part 2, "The Historiography of Airpower Theory and Doctrine," here including chapters 5–18, originally appeared in the *Journal of Military History* 64 (April 2000): 467–502. Reprinted by permission.

*ory* (Maxwell AFB, Ala.: Air University Press, 1997), is an excellent start, offering chapters on Giulio Douhet, Hugh Trenchard and the RAF, Billy Mitchell, ACTS, US naval aviators, various lesser European thinkers prior to World War II, Alexander de Seversky, the nuclear theorists of the postwar era, John Boyd, and John Warden. Furthermore, topical chapters deal with airpower in low intensity conflict, airpower and the ground battle, airpower in NATO, and Soviet air theory in the aftermath of Vietnam. The book concludes with a look ahead to space-power theory. The contributors were instructors or students at SAAS, with the exception of I. B. Holley Jr., who wrote the concluding essay. The quality of the essays, as is typical of such works, is somewhat uneven, and one notes gaps in the story—no discussion of Japanese or Chinese airpower, for example. Nevertheless, *The Paths of Heaven* is the first place to begin a study of airpower theory.

The best account of the evolution of airpower theory and doctrine in the United States is Robert Frank Futrell's *Ideas, Concepts, Doctrine: Basic Thinking in the United States Air Force,* 2 vols. (Maxwell AFB, Ala.: Air University Press, 1989), an enormously detailed, thorough, and insightful work. Futrell begins with the early days of aviation, showing how the Army began its slow and painful appreciation of the new air weapon. After reviewing the "Mitchell era" and its influence on the Air Corps and ACTS, where American air doctrine was formulated, he then examines how World War II fulfilled, modified, and in some cases rejected that doctrine. Futrell then discusses the postwar era, when the US Air Force, like the other services—indeed, the world in general—struggled to cope with the changes in war caused by nuclear weapons. He shows how the Vietnam War rudely shook these new ideas and how that war shaped modern concepts of airpower employment. No one has a better understanding of the Air Force's intellectual history than Futrell. Prodigious research went into these two volumes. Although Futrell's prose can at times be hard going, *Ideas, Concepts, Doctrine* is essential reading for anyone serious about airpower theory and doctrine.

Chapter 6

# Early Thinking

Most early writers on airpower quickly realized that aircraft would have a significant impact on military operations. Generally, they saw this impact primarily in the area of reconnaissance and communications. (That is why the first military aircraft in the United States were assigned to the Army's Signal Corps.) Examples of these early, guarded treatments include Capt G. L. Townsend's "The Use and Effect of Flying Machines on Military Operations," *Infantry Journal* 7 (September 1910): 244–59, and, more importantly, R. P. Hearne's *Aerial Warfare* (London: J. Lane, 1909). Hearne recognizes that aerial reconnaissance would have an enormous effect on armies because it would more quickly and accurately determine their positions and possible intentions: "Aircraft will destroy surprise, and therefore destroy strategy," a prescient preview of World War I. He also notes that aircraft would prove very effective in terrorizing "savage races," thus allowing easier government control in colonial possessions—another accurate prediction of how the RAF would conduct imperial policing duties during the interwar period.

Other writers were less farsighted. For example, in "The Aeroplane in War," *Harper's Weekly,* 20 August 1910 (pages 11, 36) and 27 August 1910 (pages 11–13), the usually open-minded Homer Lea asserts confidently that aircraft could never become weapons of war because their use "is incompatible with organized and stable governments." He stumbles on, finally concluding that not even reconnaissance would be possible from the air because airplanes would travel too quickly for pilots to see clearly. One finds a slightly less negative appraisal in Sir George Aston's *Sea, Land, and Air Strategy: A Comparison* (London: John Murray, 1914). Aston believes that aircraft would have little influence on war in the near term, but he does register a caveat: if in the future, aircraft numbered in the "thousands rather than the hundreds," he might change his mind. Hudson Maxim, inventor of the machine gun, also wrote about airpower in *Defenseless America* (New York: Hearst's International Library Co., 1915); contrary to most writers, he points out the physical limitations of aerial bombing. He notes, for example, the exaggerated talk of bombardment's destructiveness—bombs first had to hit the intended building, penetrate its roof, and *then* explode to cause any appreciable damage. These represented far more serious challenges than most people realized. Maxim was correct, yet amazingly few writers on the subject realized it.

F. W. Lanchester, an eclectic thinker and engineer best known for his "N Squared Laws" that attempt to predict casualties in war based on the number of participants, explains these formulas and their relation to airpower in *Aircraft in Warfare: The Dawn of the Fourth Arm* (London: Constable and Co., Ltd., 1916). In this clever and thoughtful work, Lanchester sees great strategic value in aircraft but nevertheless believes that their main importance will reside on the battlefield, where they will work in conjunction with the three other arms: infantry, artillery, and cavalry. In this regard, however, he believes that gaining air superiority is absolutely essential, and its attainment should be airpower's first priority at the outbreak of war. In words soon echoed by other air advocates, he states boldly, "The time will come when the total and irrevocable loss of the command of the air to an enemy will be regarded as a disaster of an altogether irreparable and decisive kind."

Other early writers on airpower seemed instinctively to recognize that aerial bombing would grow to dominate war, but their thoughts were inchoate and lacked specifics. In this regard, their work more closely resembled the fiction writings of H. G. Wells and Jules Verne than of military theorists. Examples of these early glimmerings of strategic thought include Claude Grahame-White's *The Aeroplane in War* (London: T. W. Laurie, 1912) and *Aircraft in the Great War: A Record and Study* (Chicago: A. C. McClurg, 1915); Frederick A. Talbot's *Aeroplanes and Dirigibles of War* (London: William Heinemann, 1915); and Edgar C. Middleton's *Airfare of To-Day and of the Future* (London: Constable, 1917).

Prior to World War II, most of the writing on airpower was surprisingly superficial and/or technical. Because of flight's status as a revolutionary development in human history, people found it fascinating but were a bit mystified as to how it actually occurred. As a result, most books on aviation began with an obligatory discussion of what makes airplanes fly, a description of lift and drag, the difficulty of directional control, the effects of rain and ice on airframes, and so forth. After these introductory chapters, authors would then begin to speculate—because they had so little empirical data to fall back on—regarding the future of aviation. Most of these speculative accounts fall into one of two categories: the boy's adventure story and the apocalyptic vision of future war. In particularly unfortunate cases, these two categories were combined under one cover—for example, Maj Gen James E. Fechet's *Flying* (Baltimore: Williams and Wilkins Co. in cooperation with the Century of Progress Exposition, 1933). Fechet, who had served as chief of the Air Corps and should have known better, wrote a distressingly bad book on airpower. One extended quote sums up the message of *Flying* as well as dozens of other such books written during the interwar years, both here and abroad:

> It takes no gazing into a crystal ball to visualize a huge trade center such as New York City completely paralyzed if not entirely destroyed, razed and depopulated in a single day by a very few flying machines. . . . Obviously the airman, riding so high above the earth that cities look like ant hills, cannot aim his deadly cargo at armed males. All below will be his impartial target. . . . The women and children and working men, extra-military, are the ones who will suffer. Extended areas will be completely depopulated. We may safely forecast that the next war will be won or lost by air effort.

This type of writing could hardly inspire people into liking airpower and seeing it as a boon to mankind. Nevertheless, airmen argued surprisingly often that airpower was a civilizing and humane instrument because it would make war so awful that it was less likely to occur. This logic is not entirely ridiculous—modern nuclear-deterrence strategy is based on the same cataclysmic image—but it involves a moral paradox that airmen have never sufficiently resolved.

Air Commodore L. E. O. Charlton, another of the prophets of doom who wrote of how air attack would turn urban populations into panic-stricken mobs, published three books, all of

101

them much the same: *War from the Air: Past, Present, Future* (London: Thomas Nelson, 1935); *War over England* (London: Longmans, Green and Co., 1936); and *The Menace of the Clouds* (London: William Hodge and Co., Ltd., 1937). This last had an unusual twist: Charlton by that point had so frightened even himself with these tales of catastrophe that he now called for worldwide air disarmament, envisioning an international air force under the aegis of the League of Nations to keep the peace. In truth, the Geneva Disarmament Conference had proposed just such an idea in 1933. But it went nowhere, and by 1937—in the face of German rearmament—the idea had become a fantasy.

Some of the better books that share the theme of the horror and inevitability of strategic bombing include G. Blanchon's *The New Warfare* (New York: Thomas Crowell, 1918); "Neon's" (pseudonym for Marion W. Acworth), *The Great Delusion: A Study of Aircraft in Peace and War* (London: E. Benn, 1927); Commander Sir Charles Dennistoun Burney's *The World, the Air and the Future* (London: Alfred A. Knopf, 1929); Stuart Chase's (translated from the French by Fred Rothwell) *Men and Machines* (New York: Macmillan, 1935); Frank Morison's (pseudonym for Albert H. Ross) *War on Great Cities: A Study of the Facts* (London: Faber and Faber, Ltd., 1937); George Fielding Eliot's *Bombs Bursting in Air: The Influence of Air Power on International Relations* (New York: Reynal and Hitchcock, 1939); and Oliver Lyman Spaulding's *Ahriman: A Study in Air Bombardment* (Boston: World Peace Foundation, 1939).

Chapter 7

# Giulio Douhet

The first person to think seriously and deeply about the role of airpower in war and then to write down those ideas, Giulio Douhet, a mechanically inclined Italian artillery officer, began writing about flight as early as 1910. Outspoken and arrogant, Douhet often found himself in conflict with his superiors. As a consequence, when war broke out in 1914, he was relegated to the infantry and assigned to an unimportant post. He nevertheless continued to agitate and write, resulting in his court-martial for insubordination in 1916. After a year in prison, he was allowed to return to duty, but little had changed. He soon retired and spent the last decade of his life writing books, articles, editorials, letters, and even novels dealing with airpower.

In 1921 Douhet published his most famous work, *Command of the Air* (first translated into English by Dino Ferrari and published by Coward-McCann in 1942; reprinted by the Office of Air Force History in 1983). It consisted of the revised version (1927) of his essay "Command of the Air"; "The Probable Aspects of the War of the Future"; a collection of letters to the editor termed "Recapitulation," which had appeared in the magazine *Rivista Aeronautica;* and "The War of 19__," a fictional account of a future war between Germany and a French-Belgian coalition. The Italian air force published another translation, by Sheila Fischer, in 1958, which reads quite differently from the Ferrari version. Fischer's edition contains "Command of the Air," "Recapitulation," a two-page summary of "The War of 19__," and three other essays not translated elsewhere. Because Douhet was the first to write about most of the important issues dealing with airpower and because most of his successors, knowingly or not, merely wrote commentaries on his ideas and predictions, I discuss Douhet's theories—and criticisms of them—in some detail.

Douhet believed that World War I had demonstrated the inevitability and totality of wars and that modern technology had produced an unbreakable stalemate on the ground. As a result, airpower—which, ironically, had helped produce the trench stalemate by removing the element of surprise—would now restore mobility to war. Because of their ability to operate in the third dimension, airplanes could fly over the trenches, mountains, and rivers that impeded armies. Moreover, they could then bomb an enemy country's "vital centers"—the key industries and structures that allowed a state to function— hitherto protected by armies and fortresses. Because aircraft could travel in any direction, at any altitude, and at any time, they would enjoy the advantage of tactical surprise. This, in turn, meant they could not be intercepted or stopped. The only defense against air attack was a good offense—countries would not attack out of fear of enemy retaliation from the air. Further, he maintained that this was such a radically new way of thinking about warfare that only trained airmen who truly understood this new weapon should be allowed to command it. Thus, one should create an independent air force—consisting primarily of self-defending bombardment aircraft—separate from the stultifying control of the army and navy.

When discussing the vital centers of a country, Douhet believed that the psychological effects of bombardment would be more pronounced than the physical effects. Consequently, he called for the use of incendiary and gas bombs (recall that combatants had used poison gas extensively in World War I) against a country's major population centers, believing that these attacks would cause such panic that the population would *demand* an end to the war. Douhet speculated that these attacks would occur before a lengthy and bloody ground battle took place. He never called for the abolition of the army and navy, but obviously he believed that in the unified defense establishment he proposed, the air force would function as the senior rather than the junior partner. As a result, he saw little need for aircraft specifically designed to assist the ground or sea battle.

Criticisms of Douhet's theories are legion. He grossly over-estimated both the physical and psychological effects of bombing. Populations did not break as quickly as he thought they would under the weight of air attack. All wars are not total wars, as the post–World War II era has repeatedly demon-

104

strated. A defense against air attack *does* exist. Ground war did *not* irrevocably stalemate: a combination of mechanization, new tactics, and airpower served to restore mobility. Of course, this meant that tactical air was not "wasteful, harmful and superfluous," as Douhet had said; rather, it was essential. Finally, legal and moral constraints *do* play a major role in war—something that has become increasingly evident over the past several decades.

Louis A. Sigaud, a true believer, wrote *Douhet and Aerial Warfare* (New York: G. P. Putnam's Sons, 1941), the first in-depth study of Douhet in English, which, predictably, had very few criticisms of the Italian general. The book is more explanation than analysis. In *Strategy in the Missile Age* (Princeton, N.J.: Princeton University Press, 1959), one of the best, though now dated, analyses of Douhet's theories, Bernard Brodie states that nuclear weapons vindicate Douhet, but this is too much of a stretch. If the only thing that makes Douhet relevant is nuclear weapons, then he is completely irrelevant.

The only biography of Douhet in English, Frank J. Cappelluti's "The Life and Thought of Giulio Douhet" (PhD diss., Rutgers University, 1967), not only gives much detail about Douhet's life but also provides an excellent description of his many writings. The only drawback to this study is its lack of critical analysis of Douhet's ideas.

A stinging critique of Douhet, reflected in its title, is Thomas Mahoney's "Doctrine of Ruthlessness," *Popular Aviation*, April 1940, 36–37, 82, 84. Maj Thomas R. Phillips published "Preview of Armageddon," a less polemical but still negative appraisal, in *Saturday Evening Post,* 12 March 1938, 12–13, 95–100. Two excellent discussions of Douhet's ideas and influence include Edward Warner's "Douhet, Mitchell, Seversky: Theories of Air Warfare," in *Makers of Modern Strategy: Military Thought from Machiavelli to Hitler,* ed. Edward Mead Earle (Princeton, N.J.: Princeton University Press, 1943) and David MacIsaac's "Voices from the Central Blue: The Air Theorists," in *Makers of Modern Strategy: From Machiavelli to the Nuclear Age,* ed. Peter Paret (Princeton, N.J.: Princeton University Press, 1986). The three most recent—and best—analyses of Douhet include Claudio Segré's "Giulio Douhet: Strategist,

105

Theorist, Prophet?" *Journal of Strategic Studies* 15 (September 1992): 69–80; Phillip S. Meilinger's "Giulio Douhet and the Origins of Airpower Theory," in *The Paths of Heaven: The Evolution of Airpower Theory* (Maxwell AFB, Ala.: Air University Press, 1997); and Alan Stephens's "The True Believers," in *The War in the Air, 1914–1994,* American ed., ed. Alan Stephens (Maxwell AFB, Ala.: Air University Press, 2001). Stephens's essay is particularly valuable because it discusses the differences and similarities between the ideas of Douhet and those of his contemporaries in Britain and the United States.

Chapter 8

# William "Billy" Mitchell

Billy Mitchell, the leading American air theorist prior to World War II, began his Army career in the Signal Corps and became more directly involved with aviation in 1915. The senior American combat air commander in World War I, he became the Air Service's chief of operations and training upon returning home in 1919. An extremely prolific writer, he published three major books on aviation, as well as dozens of articles. He wrote his first book, *Our Air Force, the Keystone of National Defense* (New York: E. P. Dutton and Co., 1921), shortly after the war; compared to his later works, it is surprisingly mild. Because Mitchell had not yet decided to launch a frontal assault on the Army and Navy, he describes airpower as a revolutionary weapon but one that would take its place alongside the other services. Foreseeing future war largely in terms of what he had just witnessed in France, Mitchell proposed using airpower as a major contributor to a land or sea campaign—not as a substitute for them.

By 1925 he had changed his views dramatically. Disgusted with what he viewed as conservatism and parochialism, he began increasingly to attack the Navy and his own superiors in the Army. In *Winged Defense: The Development and Possibilities of Modern Air Power—Economic and Military* (1925; reprint, New York: Dover, 1988), he called not only for an independent air force based on strategic bombing but also for a reduced emphasis on surface warfare. His attacks on the Navy were especially harsh.

Four years after leaving the military, his *Skyways: A Book on Modern Aeronautics* (Philadelphia: J. B. Lippincott Co., 1930), appeared. One finds little new here although by this time, Mitchell's ideas regarding the decisiveness of strategic bombing, the diminishing importance of sea power, and the need for an independent air force had become most pronounced. The articles that flowed in a steady stream from

Mitchell's pen during his life are mere fugue-like variations on a similar theme and, therefore, are of little import.

One must remember that, because Mitchell wrote to convince the American public, not his uniformed colleagues, some critics have categorized most of his published writings—with some justification—as mere propaganda and special pleading. He did, however, write an important doctrine manual, not for public consumption, that more truly reflects his ideas on how he actually believed airpower should be employed in war. *Notes on the Multi-Motored Bombardment Group, Day and Night,* written and distributed in 1922, offers a clear and lucid explanation of Mitchell's operational concepts. He states here that aircraft, although generally complementing surface operations, can at times dominate them. Especially critical of the capability of naval vessels to defend themselves from air attack, Mitchell at this stage viewed aircraft carriers favorably because of their ability to defend the fleet. Later, he would totally reject the viability of carriers, perhaps because he saw them as a threat to his goal of unifying all air assets under a separate service. Mitchell also notes the utility of strategic bombing in disrupting and possibly destroying a large portion of an enemy's war-making capability. One should note, however, that he wrote this manual prior to his climactic confrontations with his superiors, which led to his court-martial—an event that seriously radicalized his views.

Alfred F. Hurley's *Billy Mitchell, Crusader for Airpower,* new ed. (Bloomington: Indiana University Press, 1975), the best treatment of Mitchell's theories on airpower, is a well-balanced, thoroughly researched, and detailed account that also puts the airman's ideas in context, describing his activities in war and peace, personal life, and incessant arguing with his own superiors—especially the Navy. The best short treatment is Lt Col Mark A. Clodfelter's "Molding Airpower Convictions: Development and Legacy of William Mitchell's Strategic Thought," in *The Paths of Heaven: The Evolution of Airpower Theory* (Maxwell AFB, Ala.: Air University Press, 1997). See also Warner's essay in *Makers of Modern Strategy* (1943), and MacIsaac's essay in *Makers of Modern Strategy* (1986).

Chapter 9

# Air Corps Tactical School

The roots of American strategic bombing theory go back to World War I. Edgar Gorrell, an officer on the Air Service staff in France during the war, wrote a lengthy memo in November 1917 offering a theory of strategic bombing. An overlooked but remarkably prescient document, it foretold to a great extent where American air theory would go for the next 20 years. The Gorrell memo is reproduced in *The U.S. Air Service in World War I*, ed. Maurer Maurer, 4 vols. (Maxwell AFB, Ala.: AFHRA, 1978–79), 2: 141–51.

One of the earliest treatments of air doctrine's evolution in the Air Service is I. B. Holley Jr.'s *Ideas and Weapons* (New Haven, Conn.: Yale University Press, 1953). The title of this work is well chosen. Airmen are often so concerned with the development of technology and their aircraft that they neglect to carefully think through precisely what they intend to do with those aircraft once they have obtained them. Using the American experience in World War I as a case study, Holley reveals the omission of the crucial link between ideas and weapons—largely because the Air Service had no process to gather data, evaluate it, and then modify existing procedures. He argues that an appropriate doctrine-formulation process has a mechanism for surfacing and examining new ideas on airpower employment. His advice on the need to build such a process has too often been ignored, but the Air Corps Tactical School, the intellectual center of the Air Corps between the wars, definitely represented an attempt to eliminate this problem.

As with any Army branch school, airmen aspiring to higher rank and command had to attend ACTS. As a result, virtually all of the top air commanders of World War II went through the school, and many served there as instructors. Exhibiting a surprising degree of independence from the War Department hierarchy, the instructors at ACTS developed, refined, and promulgated the doctrine of high-altitude, daylight, formation, precision bombing of an enemy's industrial infrastructure.

This doctrine viewed an enemy's society as an "industrial web" with interconnected major structural components. Destroying or neutralizing key nodes within the web would affect, perhaps even paralyze, the entire system. Creating this dislocation required an air force composed of heavy bombers and commanded by airmen—after all, only someone trained and educated in the intricacies of air warfare could plan and conduct an air campaign. It was this doctrine that the Air Corps took with it into World War II.

Although some "operators" have downplayed the emphasis placed on the fairly young "thinkers" at ACTS, arguing that they have received a disproportionate share of attention simply because they wrote all the books, a close look reveals a real and significant impact. When in 1941 General Arnold, commanding general of the AAF, called for an air war plan to defeat Germany, he designated four former ACTS instructors to write it. Not coincidentally, their product, AWPD-1, looked very similar to the scenarios they had drawn up at Maxwell Field, Alabama, a few years earlier.

Robert T. Finney wrote the official history of ACTS, *History of the Air Corps Tactical School, 1920–1940,* USAF Historical Study 100 (1955; reprint, Washington, D.C.: Air Force History and Museums Program, 1998), a workmanlike administrative study useful for tracking the personnel who attended and taught there, the titles of the courses, the hours allotted to various topics, and so forth. But it gives little insight into the ideas actually discussed and formulated there. One finds a better study of the theory taught at Maxwell in Thomas H. Greer's *The Development of Air Doctrine in the Army Air Arm, 1917–1941,* Air Force Historical Study (1955; reprint, Washington, D.C.: Office of Air Force History, 1985). Although dated and lacking depth, it provides a useful starting point nevertheless. The best overall treatment to date is Lt Col Peter R. Faber's "Interwar US Army Aviation and the Air Corps Tactical School: Incubators of American Airpower," in *The Paths of Heaven: The Evolution of Airpower Theory* (Maxwell AFB, Ala.: Air University Press, 1997), a nicely written, insightful, and important treatment that clearly traces the development of strategic doctrine and places it into the contemporary context.

William Sherman, an instructor at the school in the early 1920s, wrote *Air Warfare* (New York: Ronald Press Co., 1926), one of the early treatments of ACTS theory. Largely based on his lectures, it provides insight into Air Service thinking at the time. Sherman maintained that, although potent armies would decide warfare, their success would increasingly depend upon the amount of air support they received and predicted that strategic bombing would become more important in the years ahead. Significantly, he rejected the idea of bombing population centers, calling instead for the targeting of an enemy's industrial infrastructure. Indeed, one can see in Sherman's writings an embryonic concept of the industrial-web theory fleshed out in greater detail the following decade.

Maj Gen Donald Wilson, an instructor at ACTS from 1931 to 1935, expanded Sherman's ideas. In a rather self-serving attempt to garner credit for devising the theory of industrial-web bombing, he reprinted one of his lectures "Origins of a Theory of Air Strategy," *Aerospace Historian* 18 (Spring 1971): 19–25, an excellent account of ACTS bombing theory and therefore an unusual primary source. One should keep in mind, however, that several other important officers at Maxwell at this time—specifically, Hal George, "Santy" Fairchild, Robert Webster, Larry Kuter, and "Possum" Hansell—proved instrumental in codifying this doctrine. Hansell, one of the "bomber-mafia" instructors at Maxwell and one of the authors of AWPD-1, wrote *The Air Plan That Defeated Hitler* (Atlanta: Higgins-McArthur/Longino and Porter, 1972; edited and republished by the Office of Air Force History as *Strategic Air War against Germany and Japan,* 1986), a memoir that focuses mostly on World War II and includes an interesting, informative look at ACTS during the author's tenure there. One finds it particularly effective in describing the personalities of his colleagues and their many arguments over the issues of airpower theory and employment.

In *The Foundations of US Air Doctrine: The Problem of Friction in War* (Maxwell AFB, Ala.: Air University Press, 1984), Barry D. Watts criticizes the way Air Force doctrine has developed over the decades, homing in on ACTS as the perpetrator of the original sin. Airmen have always tended to be technologically oriented in their thinking, for the obvious reason that technology is essential to their profession. The downside of this trait is the inclination to treat all obstacles as if they were engineering problems, capable of scientific analysis, measurement, and solution. This "mechanistic" view of air warfare is a big mistake, says Watts, because war is essentially a human and psychological event, and human actions are not governed by scientific laws. Thus, ACTS doctrine predicted that a measurable and predetermined amount of ordnance would produce a specific degree of destruction, which in turn would inexorably lead to a failure of the enemy's will. World War II demonstrated that this cause-and-effect linkage was not nearly so neat or obvious as expected. Watts therefore calls for a more humanistic and cultural-based method of formulating air doctrine to replace the earlier and flawed mechanistic approach.

Stephen L. McFarland's *America's Pursuit of Precision Bombing, 1910–1945* (Washington, D.C.: Smithsonian Institution Press, 1995), illuminates a very important aspect of the ACTS story. One of the key tenets of Air Corps doctrine was "precision," yet the actual bombing campaigns conducted during the war proved far less than precise. A common assertion (see Watts, above) held that ACTS thinkers merely wished away this issue in their quest to develop a theory that would separate them from ground officers. McFarland shows that this was not the case. The men at Maxwell well understood the importance of precision to the effectiveness of their operations, and they spent much time compiling data on various types of bombs, bombsights, aircraft platforms, desired altitudes, and types of targets. In a precomputer era, they nevertheless collected an enormous amount of data that lent a degree of specificity to their theories. Even if experiences in war turned out differently, ACTS personnel at least made a serious attempt to predict what their doctrine could and could not accomplish.

Unfortunately, although the works cited above give important details and insights into parts of the ACTS story, they all lack comprehensiveness and depth. We still need a complete intellectual history of this crucial institution.

The US Army had responsibility for approving Air Corps doctrine manuals, two of the most important of which included Field Manual (FM) 1-5, *Employment of Aviation of the*

*Army,* first published in April 1940 and revised in January 1943, and its successor, FM 100-20, *Command and Employment of Air Power,* published in July 1943. FM 1-5 provided a straightforward description of airpower's various strategic and tactical missions, including bombardment, interdiction, close air support, air superiority, reconnaissance, and transport. All of these missions received fairly balanced coverage, but the manual clearly emphasized airpower in support of ground operations. The far more radical FM 100-20, written after the North African campaign and dubbed the "Magna Carta of American airpower," set the tone in the first sentence: "LAND POWER AND AIR POWER ARE CO-EQUAL AND INTERDEPENDENT FORCES; NEITHER IS AN AUXILIARY OF THE OTHER" (capital letters in original). Both soldiers and airmen saw in the document the beginnings of an independent Air Force, which, in fact, became reality in 1947. One should note that the author of this manual was Larry Kuter, another of the bomber-mafia instructors at ACTS the decade before.

# Chapter 10

# **Other US Theorists**

"Hap" Arnold, the five-star commander of AAF during World War II, was a fairly prolific writer. Besides authoring six *Bill Bruce* adventure stories for boys, he also authored or coauthored four other books on airpower, plus his memoirs. His *Bill Bruce* books, all published by A. L. Burt in 1928, offer some interesting insights into life in the peacetime Air Corps. The hero, named after Arnold's young son, was an Air Corps pilot who has a number of adventures, such as flying combat during the war, patrolling forests looking for fires, and participating in the Transcontinental Reliability Test. Somewhat autobiographical, these books also speak to an era of innocence and civility that seems foreign to us today. Arnold also wrote *Airmen and Aircraft: An Introduction to Aeronautics* (New York: Ronald Press, 1926) and *This Flying Game* (New York: Funk and Wagnalls, 1936), the latter coauthored with Ira Eaker. Written for a young or unsophisticated audience, these books relate the history of flight, stories of famous airmen, training of pilots in the Army, and commercial use of airplanes—pretty routine stuff. They contain very little discussion of airpower theory as such, but that changed when Arnold and Eaker coauthored two other books: *Winged Warfare* (New York: Harper and Brothers, 1941) and *Army Flyer* (New York: Harper and Brothers, 1942). Written during World War II, they serve as primers for the layman by laying out clearly and effectively the ACTS instructors' more erudite ideas about air theory. One finds in them all of the key elements of American strategic air theory: the primacy of air superiority, airpower's inherently offensive nature, the need for centralized control of air assets by airmen, the need for a close and symbiotic relationship with the civilian aeronautical industry, the utility of transport aircraft, and, most importantly, a discussion of air targeting. Arnold and Eaker conclude that the destruction of industrial infrastructure will have profound effects on any enemy's capability and will to fight.

David E. Johnson's *Fast Tanks and Heavy Bombers: Innovation in the U.S. Army, 1917–1945* (Ithaca, N.Y.: Cornell University Press, 1998) attempts to explain the US Army's unpreparedness for World War II by focusing on what he sees as deficiencies in American doctrine for tanks and aircraft, as well as in American equipment. He identifies the culprits as intraservice parochialism and special interests. Although his treatment of the Air Corps's prewar strategic-bombardment doctrine is accurate if not original, he misses the mark on tactical airpower. Undoubtedly, tactical aviation had troubles in its baptism of fire in North Africa, but the campaign was still a success; moreover, airmen learned very quickly. By D day, American tactical air assets had become far superior to Germany's, in both quantity and quality. In short, Johnson provides an explanation for a nonexistent problem.

Although Joseph J. Corn's *The Winged Gospel: America's Romance with Aviation* (New York: Oxford University Press, 1983) is not about military aviation, much less airpower theory, I include his masterful work here because of its tangential importance to our subject. Corn has written the best account of how aviation captured the popular imagination during the first half of the twentieth century. Americans have always tended to glamorize technology and see it as a panacea for any problem, the airplane being the supreme technological example. Furthermore, one cannot ignore the almost mystical feeling that, by taking off into the pristine sky, people leave behind the world's sordidness, imperfections, and banality. Flight brings transformation and renewal. This is an important concept to understand about that more innocent age because military airmen believed that the airplane would bring about the same sort of transformation in war. Although it sounds paradoxical, people believed that the airplane, because of its ability to dominate whole countries and their populations, had made war less likely. Airpower thus exerted a civilizing and peaceful influence on the world. Later disappointments and intrusions of reality should not obscure this earlier and more benevolent vision.

Chapter 11

# The Royal Air Force

The British government reacted to German air attacks that had caused near-panic among the British population by forming the Royal Air Force on 1 April 1918. Although the German zeppelins and Gotha bombers caused only minor material damage and casualties, the psychological terror they evoked was enormous. Memories of the public's reaction to the bombing stuck in the minds of British political and military leaders throughout the interwar period and profoundly affected strategy and policy. It became an article of faith in the RAF—and, to some extent, in the British government—that strategic bombing sought to break the will of the enemy. The brief experience of the Great War seemed to indicate the attainability of such a goal. Not until the far more intensive bombing campaigns of World War II did people discover that initial panic gives way very quickly to mere fear and then to resignation.

Chosen to lead the new RAF, Hugh Trenchard, a former infantry officer who had come to aviation late in life, remained at the helm of the service from its inception until 1929, minus a brief stint as commander of the British bombing force in France at the end of the war. Termed "the father of the RAF," Trenchard has attained near-mythic proportions in the literature and traditions of the RAF for not-so-obvious reasons. He wrote little, spoke poorly, and had neither the look nor the personality of a heroic leader. Yet, within the RAF his power remained unquestioned. Although inarticulate, he had an ability to make his points clearly and forcefully to his subordinates. An early skeptic of bombing, he soon became a staunch advocate. Like Douhet, Mitchell, and ACTS, Trenchard thought that one could use strategic airpower most effectively against an enemy country's vital centers. Unlike Douhet, he rejected strikes on the general population yet called for attacks on enemy morale. He resolved this apparent paradox with an approach that differed subtly though significantly from that of the Americans. Whereas they advocated bombing the enemy's industry to destroy his *capability* to fight, Trenchard advocated bombing that industry to destroy the enemy's *will* to fight. He believed that destroying the enemy's industry, communications, transportation network, and economy would so disrupt the daily life of the working population, causing unemployment and hardship, that the people would demand an end to the war. This theory was certainly in keeping with British experience in the Great War. Given the rudimentary technology of the time, however, it soon became apparent in war that bombing accuracy made all airpower strategies, so different in theory, much the same in actual practice.

Trenchard left behind few published writings from which one can trace his thoughts. In "Aspects of Service Aviation," *The Army Quarterly* 2 (April 1921): 10–21, he lays out some of the basic ideas noted above. In addition, perhaps out of a bureaucratic imperative, he called for an air force in being that was large and modern enough to fight at the immediate outset of hostilities. The speed of aircraft and their ability to strike virtually anywhere at the inception of war had made leisurely mobilization a thing of the past. Like most other airmen, he emphasized the need for air superiority. Though a believer in the decisiveness of airpower, he cautioned against the notion that it could end war in a matter of days or weeks. Because air attack produced cumulative effects, operations had to remain persistent and continuous.

Other than memos and speeches delivered here and there, undoubtedly written by his staff officers, Trenchard did not elaborate on his ideas again until World War II. In "The Effect of the Rise of Air Power on War" (October 1943), in *Air Power: Three Papers* (London: Directorate of Staff Studies, Air Ministry, 1946), he recaps the events of war up to that time, noting that airpower played key roles in every campaign. Especially significant was the realization that the RAF's victory in the Battle of Britain had saved the country. Could airpower defeat Germany? Trenchard simply stated, "I do not know. I have never claimed that we can. Equally, I have never suggested that we cannot." He went on to argue that the Germans' industry was slowly but surely being destroyed, "which will in time render them powerless to supply their armies and Air Force in the field to carry on the war." Trenchard called for a greater effort to accomplish such destruction more quickly. In the book's two other essays, written after Germany's defeat, Trenchard merely recapitulates the key role played by the RAF in victory.

The sole biography of Trenchard, Andrew Boyle's *Trenchard* (London: Collins, 1962), though too glowing an assessment, offers rich detail and much discussion of Trenchard's thoughts on airpower. For a more focused appraisal, see my article "Trenchard and 'Morale Bombing': The Evolution of Royal Air Force Doctrine before World War II," *Journal of Military History* 60 (April 1996): 243–70.

Robin Higham's *The Military Intellectuals in Britain, 1918–1939* (1966; reprint, Westport, Conn.: Greenwood Press, 1981), a useful overall discussion of British air theory in the interwar period, contains two chapters on the RAF. The first focuses on doctrine in general, while the second deals more specifically with individuals such as P. R. C. Groves, John Slessor, E. J. Kingston-McCloughry, and James Spaight. Higham offers useful insights into the politics and inner workings of the RAF bureaucracy, but his antipathy towards Trenchard is ill disguised. Certainly we need a corrective to the hagiography of Boyle, but Higham too readily accepts the accounts of Trenchard's opponents while dismissing those of his advocates.

In his highly critical account of the RAF between the wars, *The Development of RAF Strategic Bombing Doctrine, 1919–1939* (Westport, Conn.: Praeger, 1995), Scot Robertson looks at the issue of RAF doctrine formulation and overall preparedness through the eyes of the Air Staff. As a result of this focus, his study never mentions the RAF's doctrine manuals or the educational apparatus responsible for disseminating that doctrine. Nevertheless, Robertson concludes that air leaders talked themselves into an unproven doctrinal concept based on faith and mirror imaging rather than on empirical evidence. Worse, because they had no established process for testing their doctrine, they could not identify and correct their weaknesses before the harsh realities of war swept over them.

This interpretation contains much truth. It is useful to remember, however, that, on average, the RAF received less than 15 percent of the British defense budget between the wars. Given that the other services, who received the lion's share of funds, found themselves similarly unprepared for war, it is small wonder that the paltry sums allotted to the RAF proved insufficient to ensure a first-rate force.

Several works deal with the history of the RAF and include a discussion of air theory and doctrine: Malcolm Smith's *British Air Strategy between the Wars* (Oxford: Clarendon Press, 1984); H. Montgomery Hyde's *British Air Policy between the Wars, 1918–1939* (London: Heinemann, 1976); Uri Bialer's *The Shadow of the Bomber: The Fear of Air Attack and British Politics, 1932–1939* (London: Royal Historical Society, 1980); Neville Jones's *The Beginnings of Strategic Air Power: A History of the British Bomber Force, 1923–1939* (London: Frank Cass, 1987); John James's *The Paladins: A Social History of the RAF up to the Outbreak of World War II* (London: Macdonald, 1990), a quirky but interesting treatment; Barry D. Powers's *Strategy without Slide-Rule: British Air Strategy, 1914–1939* (New York: Holmes and Meier Publishing, 1976); and Sir Charles Webster and Noble Frankland's *The Strategic Air Offensive against Germany, 1939–1945* (London: Her Majesty's Stationery Office, 1961), the first volume of the official history.

In 1922 Trenchard founded Britain's counterpart to ACTS, the RAF Staff College at Andover, calling it "the cradle of our brain." The most promising air officers and some of their brethren from the other services studied war and the role of airpower in this year-long school. Regrettably, we do not yet have an adequate history of the Staff College, largely because of clumsy record keeping at the time. A few odd pieces of lectures, exercises, and administrative notes survive in various archives, giving us only a general impression of what was taught there. The only treatment thus far is Allan D. English's article, based on his master's thesis, "The RAF Staff College and the Evolution of British Strategic Bombing Policy, 1922–1929," *Journal of Strategic Studies* 16 (September 1993): 408–31. Certainly, the subject deserves much more attention, but the limitations on sources may prove insurmountable.

Besides the Staff College, RAF officers also learned the details of their profession from official doctrine manuals. The first of these, CD-22, appeared in 1922, simply titled *Operations*. Echoing the beliefs of Trenchard, CD-22 stated that air forces must cooperate effectively with surface forces because often the object of a campaign was the destruction of the enemy's forces. In addition, the manual discussed in detail the conduct of a strategic-bombing campaign against an enemy's vital centers, with the object of both disrupting the enemy's ability to conduct war and undermining the will of its populace to continue. Replacing CD-22 in 1928, the RAF *War Manual* (AP 1300), revised several times during the next decade, was a more sophisticated effort than its predecessor, discussing airpower in a broad sense and eliminating the bulk of CD-22's organizational and administrative material. Most importantly, AP 1300 extensively discussed the rationale behind strategic bombing and the selection of targets. It is important to note that neither this manual nor any other official RAF publication ever referred to the bombing of civilian population centers. All targets suggested throughout the manual were clearly of a military nature. Like its counterpart in America, RAF doctrine differed significantly from the city-busting strategy advocated by Douhet. Interestingly, an anonymous author ("Squadron Leader"), undoubtedly an RAF staff officer, published *Basic Principles of Air Warfare (the Influence of Air Power on Sea and Land Strategy)* (Aldershot, UK: Gale and Polden, Ltd., 1927), a book that closely mirrored the official doctrine manuals, including their rejection of population bombing. We thus have a rather curious situation in which the military deliberately and vocally rejected the ideas so current and popular among the populace at the time.

Because Brig Gen P. R. C. Groves, the RAF's director of flying operations in 1918–19, was not in Trenchard's camp, his star rapidly sank in the postwar period. His well-written and thoughtful book *Our Future in the Air: A Survey of the Vital Question of British Air Power* (London: Hutchinson and Co., 1922) advocated the growing importance of strategic bombing, noting that war had now become a "war of areas" rather than of lines. He hailed airpower's ubiquity and offensive nature, putting great faith in its psychological effects. Like many airmen, he decried the lack of vision among Britain's political and military leaders, mumbling that they consistently tried to impose two-dimensional thinking on what had now become a three-dimensional world, and reserving especially strong criticism for his rival Hugh Trenchard. He repeated the message of this book in *Behind the Smoke Screen* (London: Faber and Faber, 1934).

E. J. Kingston-McCloughry, a thoughtful and serious officer who later rose to flag rank in World War II, wrote *Winged Warfare: Air Problems of Peace and War* (London: Jonathan Cape, 1937), a balanced and measured account of airpower's potential. The book mirrors the doctrine of the RAF by pronouncing the indiscriminate bombing of population centers both morally and militarily wrong. Nevertheless, Kingston-McCloughry did believe that bombing the enemy's industry established the quickest route to victory.

James M. Spaight earned a reputation as an important and influential writer, not only because of his sharp intellect and insight regarding air matters but also because of his expertise in international law. Consequently, the British government often called upon him to give an opinion on issues such as the legality of bombing certain targets. In his first book on the subject, *Aircraft in War* (London: Macmillan and Co., Ltd., 1914), he dismisses those who tried to condemn the use of aircraft in war as somehow illegal: "To question the legitimacy of the use of aircraft in war is simply to plough the sand." Spaight argues that because of the absence of international laws regulating aerial warfare, one had to fall back on those laws that governed war on land and sea. His arguments, which remained the standard interpretation for six decades thereafter, included the premise that just as artillery could indiscriminately shell a defended city to hasten its surrender, so too could airplanes bomb that city for the same purpose. Over the next three and a half decades, Spaight wrote a number of other books on the subject of airpower in war, most dealing with its legal ramifications. His most important were *Air Power and the Cities* (London: Longmans, Green, 1930), *Air Power in the Next War: A Sequel to Air Power and the Cities,*

*1930* (London: Geoffrey Bles, 1938), and *Air Power Can Disarm* (London: Air League of the British Empire in association with I. Pitman, 1948).

The most reflective, disciplined, and impressive thinker in the RAF, Wing Commander John C. "Jack" Slessor had served as a combat pilot in World War I, on Trenchard's personal staff after the war, and in various staff and command positions prior to World War II. As the RAF's director of plans just before the outbreak of war, he issued documents fraught with trenchant logic and stinging sarcasm. During the war, he served as head of Coastal Command, and in 1950 he became chief of the air staff, with the rank of Marshal of the Royal Air Force.

For our purposes, Slessor's most significant assignment occurred between 1931 and 1934, when he served as an instructor at the British Army Staff College. Although one of the staunchest of airpower advocates, his position as a teacher of soldiers made too zealous an approach counterproductive. In addition, close contact with the outstanding minds at Camberley no doubt modified his views on airpower. As a consequence, his lectures focused on a future war that postulated an expeditionary force on the Continent, as in World War I, which required close cooperation between the RAF and army. In such a scenario, Slessor recognized that strategic bombing was only tangentially related to the goals of the expeditionary force. Instead, one needed to isolate the battlefield with airpower—to disrupt and destroy the enemy's lines of supply. This mission, now called interdiction, would entail the targeting of communications and transportation nodes, fuel depots, supply and ammunition centers, and enemy field headquarters. Even so, he cautioned that the first priority, as always, remained the gaining of air superiority. Without it, ground operations would be nearly impossible. Significantly, Slessor also discussed command relationships, insisting on the equality of air and ground commanders. They should plan their operations together and then work together to implement those plans, but neither should be subordinate to the other.

Upon leaving Camberley for an assignment in India, Slessor collected his Staff College lectures and published them as the classic *Air Power and Armies* (London: Oxford University

123

Press, 1936), perhaps the most thoughtful, measured, and articulate treatise on airpower written to that time. Its emphasis on targeting the enemy's lines of supply was reflected in the Allies' "transportation plan," which proved so instrumental in disrupting German ground operations before and after D day. Similarly, his suggested command structure of coequal air and ground headquarters working side by side became accepted practice throughout the war. Higham's *The Military Intellectuals* (see above) discusses Slessor's ideas and impact; for a more thorough treatment, see my article "John C. Slessor and the Genesis of Air Interdiction," *Royal United Services Institute Journal* 140 (August 1995): 43–48.

Chapter 12

# The European Theorists

For an overview of other Europeans who thought and wrote about airpower employment, see James S. Corum's "Airpower Thought in Continental Europe between the Wars," in *The Paths of Heaven: The Evolution of Airpower Theory* (Maxwell AFB, Ala.: Air University Press, 1997). Corum argues that the Italians Amedeo Mecozzi and Italo Balbo, though usually overshadowed by their more famous countryman Giulio Douhet, had more actual influence on the Italian air force than did Douhet. He also covers events in Germany, France, and the Soviet Union prior to World War II, noting that air leaders in all three countries gave much thought to strategic bombing but, in practice, emphasized tactical aviation.

For a more in-depth look at the roots of Luftwaffe doctrine, see John H. Morrow's *Building German Airpower, 1909–1914* (Knoxville: University of Tennessee Press, 1976) and Corum's *The Luftwaffe: Creating the Operational Air War, 1918–1940* (Lawrence: University Press of Kansas, 1997). Corum and Richard R. Muller's unique and invaluable source *The Luftwaffe's Way of War: German Air Force Doctrine, 1911–1945* (Baltimore: Nautical and Aviation Publishers, 1998), a collection of translated Luftwaffe doctrine manuals and documents, provides an unusually clear and comprehensive look at the official doctrine. The authors' commentary and analysis are also very useful.

The continental background of Gen Nikolai N. Golovine, a Russian expatriate who lived and wrote in France between the wars, gave an unusual twist to his ideas, as seen in his *Air Strategy* (London: Gale and Polden, 1936). Like many airmen, Golovine was a technological determinist who believed that airpower represented the epitome of advanced technology. He especially advocated the importance of speed, with which one could not only obtain surprise but also employ as a possible antidote to air defenses. Golovine, who had an unusual amount of respect for both ground-based and airborne air defenses, perceived the growing accuracy and effectiveness of aircraft-detection systems. He even predicted the development of infrared sensors to detect aircraft at night—as well as anti-aircraft artillery. Also, unlike Douhet or Trenchard, he antici-pated an air battle, which would require escort fighters to accompany the bombers.

Chapter 13

# Naval Aviation

The peculiar demands of naval aviation and its relationship to the fleet generated some unique ideas on airpower employment. The best short treatment of this subject is David R. Mets's "The Influence of Aviation on the Evolution of American Naval Thought," in *The Paths of Heaven: The Evolution of Airpower Theory* (Maxwell AFB, Ala.: Air University Press, 1997). For more detailed treatments, see Clark G. Reynolds's *The Fast Carriers: The Forging of an Air Navy* (1968; reprint, Huntington, N.Y.: R. E. Krieger, 1978) and George W. Baer's *One Hundred Years of Sea Power: The U.S. Navy, 1890–1990* (Stanford, Calif.: Stanford University Press, 1994), excellent studies that clearly discuss the doctrinal, organizational, technical, and administrative challenges facing the US Navy during the interwar years. Due to the foresight of some exceptional individuals, the Navy was able to build an aircraft-carrier fleet second to none. Although the Navy had not codified the doctrine necessary to employ these carriers effectively as powerful, independent strike forces at the time of Pearl Harbor, it had expertly and carefully laid the groundwork. In less than a year, the service had devised and implemented the doctrine needed to employ the "fast-carrier task forces."

The British experience with naval aviation differed from that of the US Navy. From the time of the RAF's establishment in 1918, the service included all sea-based air assets previously assigned to the Royal Navy. The doctrine of the Fleet Air Arm (FAA) thus fell under the purview of the RAF, an unhappy arrangement that produced very poor results. In 1937 the FAA returned to the Royal Navy. One finds the best account of this story and the doctrine of the FAA in Geoffrey Till's *Air Power and the Royal Navy, 1914–1945: A Historical Survey* (London: Macdonald and Jane's, 1979).

# Chapter 14

# World War II and the Postwar Era

A Russian fighter pilot in World War I, Alexander P. de Seversky had emigrated to the United States near the end of the war. He formed his own aircraft company and developed some original and important designs, including the P-35 aircraft, the ancestor of the P-47 "Thunderbolt." As World War II approached, de Seversky increasingly turned his attention to writing about the use of airpower, and soon after Pearl Harbor he published *Victory through Air Power* (New York: Simon and Schuster, 1942), an enormously important book that was a huge best seller and a Book of the Month Club selection. Over five million people read it, and Walt Disney even made it into an animated motion picture.

Despite his experiences designing fighter aircraft, de Seversky had become a dedicated enthusiast of strategic bombing. Written after the battles of Norway and Crete, when airpower had dominated events on the surface, but before the costly struggle for air superiority over Germany, *Victory through Air Power* is a stark book. In it, de Seversky denigrates all suggestions of defeating Germany and Japan by relying on land and sea power—these were outmoded forms of war. Instead, long-range airpower, preferably based on American territory, would pummel the Axis powers into submission at far less cost than a land campaign and far more quickly than a sea campaign. Although filled with hyperbole and questionable logic, de Seversky's book enjoyed tremendous popularity and helped shape American public opinion on the employment of airpower.

Good contemporary critiques of de Seversky include David Brown's "Victory through Hot Air Power," *Pic,* 5 January 1943, 7–9; Hoffman Nickerson's "Seversky: 'Air Power!' Nickerson: 'Not Enough!' " *Field Artillery Journal* 32 (July 1942): 543–49; and Cy Caldwell's *Air Power and Total War* (New York: Coward-McCann, 1943). The best recent analysis of de Seversky's works is my essay "Alexander P. de Seversky and American Airpower," in *The Paths of Heaven: The Evolution of Airpower*

*Theory* (Maxwell AFB, Ala.: Air University Press, 1997). In addition, Russell E. Lee gives us important background information and insights in "*Victory through Air Power:* American Army Air Forces, Navy, and Public Reaction to the Book and Film during World War II" (master's thesis, George Mason University, 1992).

World War II brought a spate of books on the use of the new weapon. One of the first, Maj Al Williams's *Airpower* (New York: Coward-McCann, 1940), recounts the conflicts in Ethiopia, Spain, and the opening events of World War II. An "America First" supporter and opponent of President Roosevelt, Williams argues that America was woefully unprepared for war, particularly in the air—an especially serious deficiency because air had become the decisive theater of war—and called for a crash program to build up American air strength. Other books with a "victory through airpower" message appeared during the war. Like de Seversky's, they all overestimated the physical and psychological effects of bombing. Works in this category include William B. Ziff's *The Coming Battle of Germany* (New York: Duell, Sloan and Pearce, 1942); "Auspex's" *Victory from the Air* (London: Geoffrey Bles, 1941); Norman Macmillan's *Air Strategy* (London: Hutchinson and Co., Ltd., 1941); M. J. Bernard Davy's *Air Power and Civilization* (London: G. Allen and Unwin, Ltd., 1941), which deplores air bombardment yet stands in awe of its potential; Francis Vivian Drake's *Vertical Warfare* (Garden City, N.Y.: Doubleday, Doran and Co., Inc., 1943); Flight Lt V. E. R. Blunt's *The Use of Air Power* (Harrisburg, Pa.: Military Service Publishing Co., 1943); and Allan Michie's *The Air Offensive against Germany* (New York: Henry Holt and Co., 1943) and *Keep the Peace through Air Power* (New York: Henry Holt and Co., 1944).

In the aftermath of the war, a number of writers pointed to the decisive results achieved by strategic bombing over Germany and Japan. The advent of nuclear weapons strongly—for a time incontestably—reinforced this belief. Few military or political leaders stated openly that war had remained unchanged and that "the bomb" was just another weapon. Numerous books published in the decade after World War II espoused the thesis that war had forever changed and that airpower—specifically, the use of aircraft to deliver nuclear weapons—now dominated war. It seemed a safe prediction. Even the Korean War did little to shake this faith. All the services viewed Korea as an aberration. One should note that President (and former general) Dwight Eisenhower and Adm Arthur Radford, chairman of the JCS, promulgated the American policy of "massive retaliation" and did so *after* the Korean War. They hoped that airpower in the hands of the West would keep the peace through its deterrent value—a sentiment that Douhet would have understood. The concept of airpower "so horrible it was humanizing" had returned.

A book that seems to deal only tangentially with our subject, Steven T. Ross's *American War Plans, 1945–1950* (1988; reprint, London: Frank Cass, 1996), deserves special mention as a vital source because it is the most complete study to date of American war plans devised in the half decade following World War II. These war plans relied primarily on nuclear weapons delivered by air—hence, their relation to the study at hand. Soon after the war, military planners began to consider a future war against their erstwhile ally, the Soviet Union. The problems confronting these planners seemed enormous: American military forces had virtually disintegrated in the aftermath of VJ day; the Soviets maintained a huge military structure; Soviet troops dominated, if not occupied, Eastern Europe; Western Europe—our logical ally—lay prostrate; and teetering China would eventually fall to communism. Given this nightmarish scenario, planners inevitably turned towards a reliance on nuclear weapons; they would be—they would *have* to be—the equalizer in a confrontation with Soviet and Chinese mass. Ross painstakingly goes through the series of plans and their assumptions, arriving at sobering conclusions. Not only were the plans themselves ill conceived and hastily cobbled together but also they relied on a weapon—SAC's nuclear bombers—that was in fact a wooden sword. Until at least the middle of the Korean War, we had only a very small number of nuclear weapons and an equally small number of aircraft modified to carry them. To a distressing extent, our nuclear deterrent was merely a bluff.

131

The most thoughtful treatment of airpower's role in the early nuclear era is Stephan Possony's *Strategic Air Power, the Pattern of Dynamic Security* (Washington, D.C.: Infantry Journal Press, 1949). Although reluctant to put all his eggs in the nuclear basket, Possony does maintain that in a major war against the primary enemy—the Soviet Union—nuclear weapons would play the dominant role. The strength of this book lies in its clear and detailed explanation of various strategic-targeting theories. One hears that targeting is the key to airpower because, although all of an enemy country may be open to air attack, not all targets can or should be struck. Knowing which targets are more crucial than others is the essence of air strategy. Yet, air theorists have disagreed strongly over this fundamental issue. Possony discusses the pros and cons of various air-targeting schemes—population/morale, industry, fielded forces, and transportation—in a dispassionate and enlightening fashion. In truth, *Strategic Air Power* is an overlooked gem, probably the best work on airpower theory in the post–World War II era.

Marshal of the RAF Sir John Slessor, who had come a long way since *Airpower and Armies,* also wrote *Strategy for the West* (New York: Morrow, 1954), another sophisticated and impressive work that advanced the premise of "peace through nuclear airpower." It is a well-written and cogent argument for a strong nuclear air force to ensure deterrence. He followed this up with *The Great Deterrent: A Collection of Lectures, Articles, and Broadcasts on the Development of Strategic Policy in the Nuclear Age* (New York: Praeger, 1957), another book on the same theme.

Lesser works that advance a similar premise include Air Vice Marshal E. J. Kingston-McCloughry's *War in Three Dimensions: The Impact of Air-Power upon the Classical Principles of War* (London: Jonathan Cape, 1949); Alexander de Seversky's *Air Power: Key to Survival* (New York: Simon and Schuster, 1950); Asher Lee's *Air Power* (New York: Praeger, 1955); Air Marshal Sir Robert Saundby's *Air Bombardment: The Story of Its Development* (New York: Harper, 1961); and Dale O. Smith's *U.S. Military Doctrine: A Study and Appraisal* (New York: Duell, Sloan and Pearce, 1955). In his book, Smith, a serving major general in the Air Force at the time, discusses classic military theory and then explains how airpower had transformed and revitalized theories of war. George H. Quester takes an interesting approach in *Deterrence before Hiroshima: The Airpower Background of Modern Strategy* (New York: John Wiley, 1966); he recognizes that nuclear weapons were the underpinnings of deterrence policy but argues that conventional airpower played—or attempted to play—a similar role prior to World War II. He goes on to speculate about how conventional deterrence could continue to work in the nuclear age.

As the United States became increasingly embroiled in Vietnam, some people decried the turn away from massive retaliation towards "flexible response." According to them, this action effectively threw aside the West's greatest strength, and we found ourselves playing the enemy's game—one we could not win. One finds this alarmist view, reminiscent of the call for victory through airpower in World War II, in de Seversky's *America: Too Young to Die!* (New York: McGraw-Hill, 1961), even more bombastic than his earlier works; Gen Nathan F. Twining's (former chairman of the JCS), *Neither Liberty Nor Safety: A Hard Look at U.S. Military Policy and Strategy* (New York: Holt, Rinehart and Winston, 1966); and Gen Curtis E. LeMay's (with Dale O. Smith) *America Is in Danger* (New York: Funk and Wagnalls, 1968).

Chapter 15

# Vietnam and NATO

Despite the cries of the alarmists, US air doctrine remained basically unchanged, with the emphasis on strategic bombing. As a consequence, American airmen were unprepared for the type of unconventional war they had to fight in Vietnam. They had the wrong doctrine, the wrong aircraft, the wrong ordnance, the wrong training regimen, and the wrong $C^2$ system. One would have thought, therefore, that the military would have scrambled to understand this new kind of war. Such was not the case, as is demonstrated by Dennis Drew in "Air Theory, Air Force, and Low Intensity Conflict: A Short Journey to Confusion," in *The Paths of Heaven: The Evolution of Airpower Theory* (Maxwell AFB, Ala.: Air University Press, 1997). Drew traces the story of the Air Force's response to "low intensity conflict" in general and Vietnam in particular, concluding that the service gave amazingly little thought to the subject. Airmen quietly and unceremoniously seemed willing to jettison their traditional theories of air warfare, but they had little or nothing to offer in its place. Carl H. Builder confirms and elaborates upon this problem in *The Icarus Syndrome: The Role of Air Power Theory in the Evolution and Fate of the U.S. Air Force* (New Brunswick, N.J.: Transaction Publishers, 1994).

Donald J. Mrozek bluntly describes the failures of airpower doctrine in Vietnam in *Air Power and the Ground War in Vietnam: Ideas and Actions* (Maxwell AFB, Ala.: Air University Press, 1988). Another work highly critical of the Air Force's intellectual response to the Vietnam War is Lt Col David J. Dean's *The Air Force Role in Low-Intensity Conflict* (Maxwell AFB, Ala.: Air University Press, 1986). Both these works argue that the Air Force ignored the lessons of Vietnam, choosing to maintain its emphasis on expensive, complex fighter aircraft, and that its official doctrine continued to ignore low intensity conflict. David R. Mets makes a far more hopeful assessment in *Land-Based Air Power in Third World Crises* (Maxwell AFB, Ala.: Air University Press, 1986) by looking at several examples: the *Mayaguez* affair, the

Bay of Pigs, the Yom Kippur War of 1973, and various incidents in sub-Saharan Africa. He concludes that a mix of factors such as level of visibility, commitment, risk, range, destructive capability, and overall flexibility gives airpower, on balance, excellent leverage for use in future crises.

Nevertheless, the war in Vietnam did have a major effect on airmen. All the premises and assumptions of the previous four decades seemed to evaporate over the skies of North Vietnam. The primary response of airmen was to turn away from any discussion of strategic theory—it seemed to have little relevance to wars like Vietnam, and nuclear theory was now in the hands of civilian academics—to theory concerning the tactical employment of airpower. The most important of such treatments, largely because it came from a senior airman who had thought deeply on the subject, was Gen William W. Momyer's *Air Power in Three Wars* (1978; reprint, New York: Arno Press, 1980). One of the brightest officers of his generation and a fighter pilot in World War II, Momyer also commanded Seventh Air Force in Saigon during the Vietnam War. His discussion of the mechanics of tactical airpower—$C^2$, target selection, force packaging, aerial tactics, and the like—is outstanding. From this aspect, it is perhaps the best book of its kind.

Similarly, the US Army changed its focus, turning back towards the traditional Soviet enemy on the German central front. This required the Army to wash its hands of the Vietnam debacle and move on. It was more than willing to do so, and the Air Force came along too. As a result of this tacit agreement to forget the past, a close relationship began to develop between the two services. The Army devised its new doctrine of AirLand Battle, and the Air Force—although refusing to endorse this doctrine officially—was favorably disposed towards it. Harold R. Winton explores the evolution of this relationship in "An Ambivalent Partnership: US Army and Air Force Perspectives on Air-Ground Operations, 1973–90," in *The Paths of Heaven.* One can find a more detailed description of this cooperation in Donald J. Mrozek's *The US Air Force after Vietnam: Postwar Challenges and Potential for Responses* (Maxwell AFB, Ala.: Air University Press, 1988).

Obviously, the Army's new doctrine had significant implications for NATO, which meant that the alliance's air doctrine had to adjust to complement the new ground scheme. Col Maris E. McCrabb covers this evolution in "The Evolution of NATO Air Doctrine," in *The Paths of Heaven,* as does David J. Stein in *The Development of NATO Tactical Air Doctrine, 1970–1985* (Santa Monica, Calif.: RAND, 1987). In addition, Neville Brown's *The Future of Air Power* (New York: Holmes and Meier, 1986), written in the waning years of the Cold War, is an excellent mix of history, analysis, current events, and prediction that uses the NATO–Warsaw Pact confrontation as a backdrop. Unfortunately, as memory of the Cold War fades, the sheer size, mass, and geographic setting of the European central front distract the reader and distort the book's analysis. Regarding the other side of the hill, surprisingly little has appeared regarding Soviet air doctrine. For overviews, see Air Force Pamphlet 200-21, *Soviet Aerospace Handbook,* 1978, and Lt Col Edward J. Felker's "Soviet Military Doctrine and Air Theory: Change through the Light of a Storm," in *The Paths of Heaven.*

Thomas C. Schelling wrote an important book during the Vietnam era, *Arms and Influence* (New Haven, Conn.: Yale University Press, 1966), that has produced echoes ever since. An economist whose earlier works dealt with nuclear strategy and arms control, Schelling lays out the theory that came to be known as "gradual escalation." He argues that a steadily increasing use of force (one usually encounters the metaphor of a ratchet as a description of this phenomenon) can induce an adversary to modify his behavior. If the force is effective, the enemy will cease the objectionable conduct. The wielder of the ratchet may temporarily ease the pressure to allow the victim time to think things over. If necessary, one could reapply force at a slightly higher level to see if that would produce the desired results. Such a scenario presumes that the adversaries are "rational actors" who understand the signals being sent back and forth. In reality, though, war seldom fosters rational behavior. We tried Schelling's theory in Vietnam but found it wanting. Yet, the theoretical logic of his ideas has lingered; indeed, it seemed to make a comeback in the air war over Kosovo. It will be interesting to see if future policy makers will look more favorably at a strategy of gradual escalation.

Chapter 16

# The Current Debate

The rest of the world did not remain idle while the United States endured the agony of Vietnam and then recovered from it. In Australia, airmen faced a problem not unlike the one the United States faced in the years prior to World War II: how to defend a large country with a very long coastline on a modest budget. The Royal Australian Air Force (RAAF) posited a need for long-range, mobile, and flexible strike forces—qualities that obviously pointed towards airpower. The RAAF boasted a vigorous and intellectually active core of individuals who thought and wrote seriously about the role of airpower in Australian defense. One of them, Group Capt Gary Waters, wrote *The Architect of Victory: Air Campaigns for Australia,* Canberra Papers on Strategy and Defence no. 74 (Canberra, Australia: Australian National University, 1991), which emphasized three distinct but interrelated air campaigns that would prove necessary in the event of war: the "prime" campaign for air superiority, the "separate" campaign of strategic bombardment, and the "force-multiplier" campaign of air cooperation with surface forces. Without the most important of these, the air-superiority campaign, all military operations would find themselves in dire straits. Waters provides an excellent discussion of air superiority and ways of achieving it. He describes in detail the difference between defensive and offensive counterair operations, the former relying largely on passive measures such as air patrols and ground defenses and the latter more aggressively focusing on efforts to seek out and destroy the enemy air force. Waters identifies the strengths and weaknesses of each and discusses circumstances and situations in which one might become more desirable than the other. Overall, *The Architect of Victory* is an excellent book with an Asian perspective.

Air Commodore Jasjit Singh of the Indian air force presents another unusual and important view in his clear and forceful book *Air Power in Modern Warfare* (New Delhi: Lancer, 1985), in which he stresses the importance of maintaining an offensive spirit so as to continually induce psychological and dynamic shock in an enemy. In this regard, however, he emphasizes the importance of air interdiction, arguing that the effectiveness of strategic air attacks is debatable; he also sees only limited utility in close air support, at the other end of the spectrum. He states that economy of force remains one of airpower's greatest attributes—its ability to focus great power quickly in a specific area—and that one should not waste it on targets which can be handled by other means, such as artillery or armored forces. Foreseeing land forces becoming more supportive of air operations, rather than the other way around, Singh declares that soldiers have begun to realize this change although they will not acknowledge it publicly. Overall, *Air Power in Modern Warfare* is a most interesting book from a different perspective.

Rear Adm James A. Winnefeld and Dana J. Johnson examine the specific issue of $C^2$ of all air assets in a given theater, a thorny issue for decades, in *Joint Air Operations: Pursuit of Unity in Command and Control, 1942-1991* (Annapolis: Naval Institute Press, 1993). Given not only the normal interservice rivalry that routinely exists but also the added complication of differing views on airpower between airmen of different services, this problem should not come as a surprise. The authors examine a series of case studies—Midway, Guadalcanal, Korea, Vietnam, and Desert Storm—to illustrate how these differences of opinion and focus have negatively affected air operations. Their suggested solution involves a call for an air component commander in charge of all air assets in-theater—Air Force, Navy, Marine, Army, and allied—in order to more efficiently and effectively apply generally limited but highly potent air assets. They argue convincingly that in times of fiscal austerity, which usually occur after every war, services tend to become overly defensive and wary about their prerogatives; but the new environment will not allow such parochialism. "Jointness" is the new watchword for future air operations.

Anything by Air Vice Marshal R. A. "Tony" Mason will be of interest since he is one of the most intelligent, rigorous, and creative airpower thinkers we have today. In *Air Power: A Cen-*

*tennial Appraisal* (London: Brassey's, 1994), Mason covers a wide area. Indeed, it is neither, as the title suggests, an over-all treatment of airpower in all of its various roles worldwide nor an assessment of how well airpower has performed in war. Instead, it is a somewhat disparate collection of essays that, although excellent, have no centralizing theme. Nevertheless, one finds some true gems here; my favorites are the chapters on arms control in the 1980s and the concluding chapter "The Era of Differential Airpower," a look to the future of airpower in the post–Cold War era.

Mason's colleague and countryman Air Commodore Andrew G. B. Vallance wrote an overview of air warfare titled *The Air Weapon: Doctrines of Air Power Strategy and Operational Art* (New York: St. Martin's Press, 1996). Like Mason, Vallance had served as the RAF's director of defence studies, charged with thinking about airpower theory and doctrine, helping to evolve it, and then disseminating it throughout his service. This book is the culmination of those efforts. Vallance states boldly that airpower today dominates military operations and that this dominance will likely continue for the foreseeable future. Paradoxically, most airmen—to say nothing of the other serv-ices and the public—do not adequately understand what air-power can and cannot do. Vallance, therefore, has written a primer that discusses the fundamental characteristics of air-power and then explains in detail its various roles and mis-sions, such as air superiority, antisurface attack, strategic attack, and air transport. The strength of this presentation lies more in its clarity than in any new insights.

In the United States, conventional strategic-airpower theory had been throttled both by reliance on nuclear weapons and, at the other extreme, by the largely tactical nature of the Viet-nam War. This began to change with the work of Col John Boyd, a fighter pilot at the Air Force's Fighter Weapons School. Intrigued by the astounding success of the F-86 in air combat with the MiG-15 (a 10-to-one superiority) during the Korean War, he decided that the F-86's advantage was due largely to its hydraulically operated flight controls and all-flying hori-zontal stabilizer, which allowed it to change from one aerial maneuver to another more rapidly than the MiG. After further thought, Boyd saw broader implications of this theory. The key to victory lay in acting more quickly, both mentally and physically, than one's opponent. He expressed this concept in a cyclical process he called the OODA (observe-orient-decide-act) Loop. As soon as one side acted, it observed the consequences, and the loop began anew. The most important portion of the loop was the "orient" phase. Boyd speculated that the increasing complexities of the modern world necessitated an ability to take seemingly isolated facts and ideas from different disciplines and events, deconstruct them to their essential components, and then put them back together in new and unusual ways. He termed this process "destruction and creation," which dominated the orient phase of his OODA Loop.

Significantly, Boyd later hypothesized that this continuously operating cycle applied not only in an aerial dogfight but also at the higher levels of war. In tracing the history of war, Boyd saw victory consistently going to the side that could think more creatively—orienting itself—and then act quickly on that insight. Although military historians tend to blanch at such a selective use of history, the thesis is interesting. Because of the emphasis on the orientation phase of the loop, in practical terms, Boyd was calling for a strategy directed against the mind of the enemy leadership. Although posited by an airman, these theories encompassed far more than a blueprint for air operations. Warfare in general was governed by this process. Nevertheless, because of the OODA Loop's emphasis on speed and the disorienting surprise it inflicts on the enemy, Boyd's theories seem especially applicable to airpower, which embodies these two qualities most fully.

Boyd never published his theories. Instead, he presented a several-hours-long briefing, consisting of hundreds of slides, titled "A Discourse on Winning and Losing," generally accompanied by an eight-page typescript titled "Destruction and Creation." (Most staff college and war college libraries have Xerox copies of the briefing.) Because the examples Boyd pulled from military history to support his theories are highly selective, one must view his entire edifice with great caution. Although he is cited frequently as a guru of maneuver warfare, we have surprisingly few critical analyses of his theories. The best critique thus far is Lt Col David S. Fadok's "John Boyd and John Warden: Airpower's Quest for Strategic Paralysis," in *The Paths of Heaven: The Evolution of Airpower Theory* (Maxwell AFB, Ala.: Air University Press, 1997).

Col John Warden also has thought deeply on strategic airpower and has focused on enemy leadership as the key target set. Like Boyd, a fighter pilot and combat veteran, Warden began a serious and sustained study of air warfare as a student at the National War College in 1986. The thesis he wrote that year soon saw publication and remains a standard text at Air University: *The Air Campaign: Planning for Combat* (Washington, D.C.: Pergamon-Brassey's, 1989). Although this book has had a major impact on Air Force thinking, its calls for strategic airpower are relatively modest. That would come later. A subsequent assignment in the Pentagon put Warden in an ideal location when Saddam Hussein invaded Kuwait in April 1990. Putting his theories into practice, Warden designed an air campaign that called for strategic attacks against Iraq's centers of gravity. To illustrate his plan, he used a target figure consisting of five concentric rings, with leadership at the center—the most important target but also the most fragile—and armed forces as the outermost ring—the least important but also the most hardened. Warden posited that the enemy leader represented the key to resistance—killing, capturing, or isolating him would incapacitate the entire country. Warden explains this model in his essays "Employing Air Power in the Twenty-first Century," in Richard H. Shultz Jr. and Robert L. Pfaltzgraff Jr.'s *The Future of Air Power in the Aftermath of the Gulf War* (Maxwell AFB, Ala.: Air University Press, 1992), and "The Enemy as a System," *Airpower Journal* 9 (Spring 1995): 40–55. Of interest, Warden has coauthored another book with Leland A. Russell, *Winning in Fast Time: Create the Future with Prometheus* (New York: HarperCollins, 2001), in which he attempts to translate his ideas on air-campaign planning and war fighting to the commercial sector. Using historical examples and drawing on his previous writings on air theory, Warden provides a formula for success in the business world. For our purposes, the book's utility lies in the additional insight it provides into Warden's ideas on planning and strategy at the macrolevel. One can find an excellent analysis and critique of Warden's ideas in Fadok's essay in *The Paths of Heaven,* mentioned above. David R. Mets's *The Air Campaign: John Warden and the Classical Airpower Theorists* (Maxwell AFB, Ala.: Air University Press, 1999) places Warden in the broader context of airpower theory.

Apparently, both Boyd and Warden turned away from the economic emphasis of previous airpower theorists, focusing instead on the enemy's leadership. However, whereas Boyd seeks to disrupt the process of that leadership, Warden wishes to disrupt its form. The Gulf War was the epitome of such an air strategy. Air strikes against the Iraqi communications network, road and rail system, and electrical power grid made it extremely difficult for Saddam to physically control his military forces; they also infused his decision-making process with enormous confusion and uncertainty. His OODA Loop expanded dramatically, and its cycle time slowed accordingly. For an excellent discussion that takes the ideas of Boyd and Warden to a higher level, see Maj Jason Barlow's *Strategic Paralysis: An Airpower Theory for the Present* (Maxwell AFB, Ala.: Air University Press, 1994).

Robert A. Pape proposes a counter to the idea of targeting leadership in *Bombing to Win: Air Power and Coercion in War* (Ithaca, N.Y.: Cornell University Press, 1996). A social scientist well versed in the models and methodologies of that discipline, Pape has adopted the lexicon that talks of war strategies in terms of coercion, denial, punishment, and risk. Basically, the coercion school argues that the key to victory lies in affecting the mind of the enemy, who must be convinced that victory is impossible or would cost too much to achieve. Denial strategy, on the other hand, focuses on an enemy's capability. If an enemy is disarmed, the question of whether or not his will is broken becomes irrelevant. Theoretically, the choice of coercive versus denial strategy will have a great impact on the types of targets selected by an air planner. In practice, however, it is difficult to separate targets so cleanly: almost every target will have both a coercive and denial effect on an enemy. The issue thus becomes one of emphasis. Boyd and Warden come down on the side of coercion, whereas Pape believes in denial.

In Pape's theory, the object of war remains what it has been for centuries—destruction of the enemy army, which renders a country defenseless and likely to surrender. Only now, says Pape, air forces can kill armies faster and easier than armies can kill armies. Using examples from World War II, Korea, Vietnam, and the Persian Gulf War, he argues that coercion does not work, but denial does. The main criticism of Pape's theory centers on his methodology. As noted above, it is virtually impossible to separate coercion targets from denial targets. All the wars that Pape discusses obviously employed both types of strategies simultaneously, thus preventing confirmation of the opinion that, for example, Saddam Hussein surrendered because his army in Kuwait was being destroyed. By the same token, however, one finds it equally impossible to argue that surrender occurred because of the effects of air attacks on Iraq's industry, power network, transportation, or communications networks—arguments made by John Warden and others.

Although this issue poses questions that may be unanswerable, it in no way lessens the vigor of the debate. A series of articles written by Pape, Warden, Barry Watts, and Karl D. Mueller that appeared in the 1997 and 1998 issues of *Security Studies* makes for fascinating and stimulating reading. Although the bottom line on this debate seems to cast doubt on *any* monocausal factor in victory—war is simply too complex to become that reductive—the spirit and depth of intellectual discourse over the past several years have proven extremely valuable. Frankly, airpower has become an increasingly important policy tool in the past decade, as evidenced in Iraq, Bosnia, and Kosovo. Thus, a dialogue that seriously discusses the most effective method of employing airpower would benefit our national defense.

*Strategy, Air Strike and Small Nations* (Canberra, Australia: Aerospace Studies Centre, 1999), by Wing Commander Shaun Clarke of the New Zealand air force, is an unusually fresh and original treatment. Because most current writings about airpower come from the pens of "large-nation" airmen, Clarke questions their applicability to the air arms of the world's 129 "small nations" that possess an air-strike capability. He therefore sets about examining the issue of strategic air attack and its relevance to a New Zealand–Australian alliance that possesses 150 strike aircraft. In the past decade, the emergence of highly effective and increasingly inexpensive PGMs has made strategic air strikes exponentially more effective than they were previously. The question then becomes one of targeting—and Clarke favors the leadership school. He coins a term, "SPOT (strategic persuasion oriented targeting) bombing," which employs a detailed intelligence assessment of an adversary and utilizes PGMs to produce the maximum effect on enemy leadership. Of course, one encounters problems with the leadership model—there is precious little empirical evidence to show how, or even if, such a targeting strategy will work. Theoretically, the concept is logical, but in practice, only a few times in history has a leadership change led to a change of policy benefiting the attacker.

Nevertheless, his basic theme is inherently useful and important. Small nations have limited resources with which to gain their ends. Because every shot must count, their air planners must—without fail—focus, define, and prioritize. Precision attack by air now offers substantial opportunities for small powers because it combines low risk with low cost to achieve large results. *Strategy, Air Strike and Small Nations* is fascinating reading for all planners, strategists, and airmen. For Americans, grappling with the problems of small nations— whether allies or adversaries—and understanding how they address issues of air warfare can be a very rewarding process.

Daniel L. Byman, Matthew C. Waxman, and Eric Larson's *Air Power as a Coercive Instrument* (Santa Monica, Calif.: RAND Corporation, 1999), an excellent overview that is broader and less doctrinaire than Pape's or Warden's, notes several factors that help lead to successful coercion by using airpower: achieving "escalation dominance," negating the adversary's strategy, and bringing third parties to bear to leverage or frighten the coerced party. If readers can get past such elements of the social-science lexicon, they will see that the authors' ideas are first rate. They argue that the geopolitical environment of the new century will emphasize—at least for the West—the lack of major threats to national interests, coalition operations, the increasing role of nonstate actors, and a growing concern for minimizing casualties—on both sides. In such an environment, the coercive use of airpower should grow in importance.

Benjamin S. Lambeth's *The Transformation of American Airpower* (Ithaca, N.Y.: Cornell University Press, 2000) is an excellent overview of air warfare during the last decade of the twentieth century. Lambeth actually begins with a look at how the Vietnam War shook the faith of airmen in their chosen weapon. We made many mistakes in that war, and although some military leaders would blame them on the politicians, the author shows that the Air Force accepted its part of the blame. Consequently, it began to transform itself—far more thoroughly than did the other services—into a service that employed stealth aircraft and PGMs, and invested heavily in space-based command, control, communications, computers, intelligence, surveillance, and reconnaissance ($C^4ISR$) assets that dominated the Persian Gulf War in 1991 and the conflicts with Serbia that followed. In Lambeth's words, "American airpower now possesses the wherewithal for neutralizing an enemy's military means not through the classic imposition of brute force, but rather through the functional effects achievable by targeting his key vulnerabilities and taking away his capacity for organized military action." That is, airpower is approaching a situation dreamed of by war theorists like J. F. C. Fuller and B. H. Liddell Hart prior to World War II—paralysis of the enemy. This signals a significant move away from the annihilation and attrition models of the past.

Lambeth's analysis of the air war over Kosovo is particularly compelling, giving a balanced and insightful appraisal that covers the bad along with the good. He warns that political guidance during the war, as well as NATO's decision-making process, was weak, inconsistent, and cumbersome. NATO airpower saved a bad situation, but we need to address the systemic political problems witnessed in 1999 to avoid putting an unreasonable burden on air forces in the future.

Chapter 17

# Anthologies on Modern Airpower

Both the RAF and the RAAF have periodic conferences where international scholars and serving officers gather to present papers, debate, and exchange ideas on airpower employment. Often, the papers are published. As with all such collections, one finds some chaff along with the wheat: some of the papers tend to be poorly written, researched, or argued. Others are focused so narrowly that they have little utility and longevity. But other papers are excellent, and they make these books worthwhile.

One such compendium, *The Future of United Kingdom Air Power,* ed. Philip Sabin (London: Brassey's Defence Publishers, 1988), focuses on the British situation but also discusses the employment of naval aviation. Regrettably, "land" airmen and "water" airmen too often become adversarial and parochial; indeed, they generally have little to do with one another. This is unfortunate, so including this topic here is important. Other volumes in this series—if we may call it that—include *Air Power: Collected Essays on Doctrine,* ed. Group Capt Andrew Vallance (London: Her Majesty's Stationery Office, 1990) and three excellent compendiums edited by Alan Stephens, head of the RAAF's Air Power Studies Centre: *Smaller But Larger: Conventional Air Power into the 21st Century* (Canberra: Australian Government Publishing Service, 1991); *Defending the Air/Sea Gap* (Canberra: Australian Defence Studies Centre, 1992); and *New Era Security and the RAAF* (Fairbairn: Air Power Studies Centre, 1996). Under the enlightened guidance of Stephens, the Australians have done most impressive work. Every one of these volumes contains several thought-provoking essays that look at airpower in a unique and interesting way. The most recent effort from the RAAF is *Airpower and Joint Forces,* ed. Wing Commander Keith Burt (Canberra: Aerospace Studies Centre, 2000), whose title provides the focus of this work, which contains a number of excellent essays by Richard P. Hallion on asymmetric threats, Stephen Badsey on the media,

Brig Gen David Deptula on air-exclusion zones, Alan Stephens on command and leadership, and Ian McFarland on ethics and the airman. *The Dynamics of Air Power,* ed. Group Capt Andrew Lambert and Arthur Williamson (Bracknell: Royal Air Force Staff College, 1996) has some particularly interesting and useful essays on airpower and coercion by Michael Clarke, the role of the media in air operations by Wing Commander Mike Bratby, and several that deal with airpower in peace-enforcement operations.

*Perspectives on Air Power: Air Power in Its Wider Context,* ed. Group Capt Stuart Peach (London: The Stationery Office, 1998), an intriguing collection published by the RAF, has an interesting thread that runs throughout. Warfare is becoming increasingly joint, not only because of organizational imperatives but also because airpower has permeated all the services to such a great extent. In the United States, for example, the Army, Navy, and Marine Corps all have air arms that are among the largest and most capable in the world. At the same time, however, the Navy has its own land force of marines, the Army has its own fleet of supply ships, and all of the services rely heavily on space assets. In addition, the debate over strategic versus tactical air has separated airmen from their surface brethren for decades. Over the past decade, however, surface forces have become far more interested in the "deep battle"—an area they considered unimportant because they could not reach it before. As these forces steadily encroached into what had been "air territory," airmen turned towards targeting strategies that have focused on $C^2$ networks, fielded forces, and leadership nodes. In short, the views of all the services are beginning to focus on the same area, thus facilitating a more comprehensive and complementary approach to war fighting.

The latest edition in this series is *Airpower 21: Challenges for the New Century,* ed. Group Capt Peter W. Gray (London: The Stationery Office, 2000). Michael Clarke, David Gates, and Tony Mason all discuss the changing political climate in which airpower must now be employed. Because airpower now seems to offer the greatest likelihood of achieving political goals at minimum cost, it has become the weapon of choice. However, given the lack of a serious threat to most NATO countries, politicians recognize that any use of force depends upon an unpredictable and possibly fickle public. To ensure domestic support, politicians will therefore exercise close control of any military operation. Air commanders must expect increased scrutiny of their actions—what many in the service would consider micromanagement or meddling. Mason further notes that the hated nonstrategy of "gradual escalation" may see employment more often in the future. Although failing miserably in Vietnam, it seemed to achieve some success over Kosovo. Because this approach allows close political control throughout a crisis, it may prove irresistible for political leaders—always wary of public opinion.

Philip Sabin lists possible asymmetric strategies and tactics that an enemy might employ to overcome our airpower advantage—after all, future adversaries probably won't be so foolish as to fight us on our own terms. Sir Timothy Garden takes an insightful look at European airpower, noting that Europe as a whole is as wealthy as the United States but spends far less on defense. Worse, Europe's defense funding is terribly unbalanced. It possesses far too many ground troops—nearly twice that of the United States, counting all reserve forces—yet has little intention of ever using such high-risk forces. Garden calls for a decrease in troop levels and a corresponding increase in spending on high-tech weapons to keep pace with US advances. In addition, he notes that European air arms are also unbalanced—they have too many aircraft devoted to air defense and too few to attack. During the Cold War, when the Warsaw Pact posed a serious threat, this mix made sense—but no longer. In addition, airlift and tanker forces, though copious, are poorly managed. He suggests a system similar to that which governs airborne warning and control system aircraft: the airframes are pooled, perhaps even owned by NATO, and used efficiently to service all the member nations.

Other anthologies include *War in the Third Dimension: Essays in Contemporary Air Power,* ed. Tony Mason (London: Brassey's Defence Publishers, 1986), an excellent collection that includes truly outstanding essays by Mason himself on the air-superiority campaign, David MacIsaac on the evolution of American air doctrine after World War II, Alan Gropman on the air war in Vietnam, and Ben Lambeth on Soviet air doctrine and practice. Another outstanding effort is *Air Power Confronts an Unstable World,* ed. Richard P. Hallion (London: Brassey's Defence Publishers, 1997). Hallion, himself an excellent historian and the US Air Force historian, has assembled a worthy stable of airpower thinkers and writers. One finds some truly seminal essays here by Barry D. Watts on technology, Group Capt Andrew Lambert on the psychological effects of air attack, Rear Adm James A. Winnefeld on joint air operations, Hallion himself on the importance of the revolution in precision weapons, Col Phil Meilinger on air-targeting strategies, Alan Stephens on restructuring air forces after the Cold War, and Fred Frostic on the revolution in military affairs occasioned by airpower and its effect on future war. *War in the Third Dimension* is the best airpower anthology to date—the standard by which other such efforts should be judged.

Gen Merrill A. "Tony" McPeak, the Air Force chief of staff during the Persian Gulf War and the four years that followed, did something after his retirement that no other chief has done—collected and published the key speeches, briefings, and press releases from his tenure as chief. This was a terrific idea. Although some of the topics deal with contemporary events of decreasing importance today—Air Force reorganization, personnel policies, gays in the military, and sexual harassment in the wake of the Navy's Tailhook scandal—some discuss significant and timely issues. McPeak led the Air Force during its most tumultuous period in decades, overseeing a downsizing of nearly one-third, which caused him to think through basic questions regarding the mission, vision, purpose, organization, and force structure of the Air Force. Included in this collection, *Selected Works, 1990–1994* (Maxwell AFB, Ala.: Air University Press, 1995), are his "mother of all briefings" to the press corps following the victory in Desert Storm, the "mission of the Air Force" dinner address, and various speeches that outline his thoughts on the future of airpower. Perhaps most importantly, this work contains McPeak's views on future war. He advocated the division of war into three distinct battles: close, deep, and high (air and space). In his view, surface forces predominate in the close battle, and airpower supports the ground commander in that regime. In the high and deep battles, however, McPeak argues that air and space assets dominate; hence, airmen should command these battles, with surface forces in support. Despite the clear and obvious logic of his argument, the other services did not welcome his ideas, immediately closing ranks to condemn them. As McPeak himself admitted, he advocated "taking away too many of their rice bowls." Nevertheless, with the passing of time, his vision is evolving into reality.

Chapter 18

# Conclusion

The body of literature surrounding airpower theory is fairly large but uneven in quality. It is surprising that so much has been written about a new kind of war that has existed for such a short time. After all, it took millennia to produce a Carl von Clausewitz and an Alfred Thayer Mahan. Still, one notices some broad gaps. Someone needs to write the definitive history of the Air Corps Tactical School and its impact on the employment of American airpower in World War II. Pieces of this story are scattered about, but ACTS was so important that it demands a fuller treatment. Similarly, the counterpart of ACTS in Britain, the Royal Air Force Staff College, needs some attention. No one knows whether the Staff College played as crucial a role in the RAF as ACTS did in the Air Corps, but even proving the negative would be useful. I suspect, however, that the Staff College played a key part in the story and did have enormous influence in formulating and then disseminating air doctrine, not only throughout the RAF but also throughout the empire.

Along these lines, no one has sufficiently explored the ideas of Hugh Trenchard and Jack Slessor. Both men left behind enormous amounts of material that beg for the attention of researchers. Trenchard has had only one biographer and Slessor none, and their theories have attracted only scattered articles. Much work remains to be done on these two figures.

Giulio Douhet has also been neglected, partly because of language difficulties. Surprisingly few of his many writings have been translated into English. For example, it would be fascinating to explore the articles on aviation he wrote as early as 1910—to discover what his thinking was at that time. He also carried on extensive correspondence with military contemporaries, aircraft builders, and magazines. The essay "Recapitulation," which appears in translations of *Command of the Air* contains only Douhet's responses to criticisms—the criticisms themselves have never been translated and pub-

155

lished. Douhet also kept an extensive, untranslated diary during World War I. Finally, and most intriguingly, the 1921 edition of *Command of the Air* contained a 100-page appendix that did not appear in the 1927 version—it too remains untranslated. A huge lode of material needs to be mined. One can easily imagine a multivolume project containing the collected writings of Giulio Douhet.

Language barriers have also limited our understanding of French, Japanese, Russian, and—to a lesser extent—German airpower thinkers, especially in the interwar period. Because of the paucity of translations of primary material from that era, one suspects that what has been written about the air arms of these countries lacks depth and sufficient analysis.

Gen Tony McPeak's idea of collecting and publishing his most important speeches is truly outstanding. All future chiefs should follow his example. In addition, however, someone should make a serious attempt to collect and then publish the most significant addresses and papers of former air leaders. To be able to read how air commanders in Korea, Vietnam, Desert Storm, and Kosovo, for example, viewed the mission and how they learned various lessons from the conflicts in which they played key roles would be invaluable.

The most encouraging development of late has been the great resurgence of interest in and debate on airpower issues. New technologies such as precision weapons, stealth, and electronic sensors have dramatically altered the way air forces fight. This, in turn, has spawned a debate of unusually high tone and sophistication. One can only hope that this trend will continue.

# Glossary

| | |
|---|---|
| AAF | Army Air Forces |
| AB | air base |
| ACTS | Air Corps Tactical School |
| AFHRA | Air Force Historical Research Agency |
| AWPD | Air War Plans Division |
| $C^2$ | command and control |
| $C^4ISR$ | command, control, communications, computers, intelligence, surveillance, and reconnaissance |
| CAT | Civil Air Transport |
| CIA | Central Intelligence Agency |
| FAA | Fleet Air Arm |
| FEAF | Far East Air Forces |
| FM | field manual |
| GHQ | General Headquarters |
| JCS | Joint Chiefs of Staff |
| MAC | Military Airlift Command |
| NATO | North Atlantic Treaty Organization |
| NORAD | North American Air Defense Command |
| OODA | observe-orient-decide-act |
| PGM | precision-guided munition |
| RAAF | Royal Australian Air Force |
| RAF | Royal Air Force |
| R&D | research and development |
| ROTC | Reserve Officer Training Corps |
| SAAS | School of Advanced Airpower Studies |
| SAC | Strategic Air Command |
| SACEUR | supreme allied commander Europe |
| TAC | Tactical Air Command |
| UN | United Nations |
| USSTAF | US Strategic Air Forces |

# Index

strategic airpower, 9, 20, 23, 32, 42, 48–49, 58, 115, 117, 141, 143
strategic bombing, 21, 30–31, 34, 38, 41, 43–44, 52, 62–63, 68, 102, 107–9, 111, 117, 119–21, 123, 125, 130, 139
strategic doctrine, 14, 43, 110, 116
strategy, 3, 6, 20, 23, 26, 36, 40–41, 44, 47, 54, 60–62, 68, 70, 87, 99, 101, 105, 108, 111, 117, 120–21, 125, 130, 132–33, 137–39, 141–46
Stratemeyer, George E., 66–67
supreme allied commander Europe (SACEUR), 68–70
Symington, Stuart, 3, 32

Tactical Air Command (TAC), 42, 49, 92
tactical airpower, 27, 39, 50, 63, 116, 136
targeting, 23, 47, 111, 115, 123–24, 132, 143–44, 146–47, 150, 152
Taylor, Maxwell D., 61
technology, 21–22, 26, 29, 93, 103, 109, 111, 116, 118, 152, 156
Tedder, Arthur, 57
Tenth Air Force, 46
Tet offensive, 76
Thirteenth Air Force, 58, 72
384th Bomb Group, 55
322d Group, 72
Tinker, Clarence L., 16
Towers, John H., 18–19, 24
Trenchard, Hugh, 98, 117–23, 126, 155
Truman, Harry S., 49, 51, 53
Tunner, William H., 64–66
Tuskegee airmen, 71, 73–74
Twelfth Air Force, 29, 51, 80
Twentieth Air Force, 38, 42–43, 58, 68, 71, 78, 97, 116, 147
XXI Bomber Command, 42–43
Twining, Nathan F., 58–59, 79, 85–87, 91–92, 133

unconventional war, 135
United Nations (UN), 57, 66
United States Air Forces Europe, 68
unmanned air vehicles, 22
US Strategic Air Forces (USSTAF), 32, 34

US Strategic Bombing Survey, 52
US Strike Command, 72

Vandenberg, Arthur, 38
Vandenberg, Hoyt S., 37–38, 45, 50–52, 58–61, 79, 85–87, 91–92
Vietcong, 62
Vietnam, 61–62, 70, 72–74, 76–82, 86, 88, 91–92, 98, 133, 135–37, 139–41, 145, 147, 151–52, 156
vital centers, 9, 104, 121
VJ day, 131

Walker, Kenneth N., 40–41
Wallace, George, 61
Warden, John, 82, 98, 143–46
War Department, 13, 34, 51, 53, 109
Warner Robins Army Air Depot, 26
Warsaw Pact, 151
Weapons Systems Evaluation Group, 42
Webster, Robert, 111
Welch, Larry, 92
Westmoreland, William C., 76
Westover, Oscar M., 15, 20
West Point, 5, 19, 21, 25, 35, 50, 54–55, 57, 59, 66, 68, 71–72, 78, 81
Weyland, Otto "Opie," 91
Wheeler, Earle, 78
Wheelus AB, Libya, 73
Whitehead, Ennis, 44–45
White, Thomas, 61, 78, 91
Wilson, Donald, 40, 111
World War I, 6, 8–9, 12, 14–15, 20, 22, 32, 36, 39, 46, 52–53, 58, 103–4, 107, 109, 123, 129
World War II, 10, 16, 23, 31–32, 35–36, 40–41, 43, 46–50, 53–54, 59, 65, 69, 71, 74–75, 78, 87, 91–92, 98, 100, 107, 109, 111–12, 115–17, 119–20, 122, 125, 129–31, 133, 136, 139, 145, 147, 152
Wright brothers, 13–14, 19, 87
Wright Field, Ohio, 7, 25, 36

Yalta conference, 35–36
Yeager, Chuck, 3
Yom Kippur War, 136

Zuckert, Eugene, 63

# Airmen and Air Theory

## A Review of the Sources

*Cover Design*
Phil Meilinger

*Air University Press Team*

*Chief Editor*
Marvin Bassett

*Copy Editor*
Carolyn J. McCormack

*Book Design and Cover Art*
Steven C. Garst

*Composition and
Prepress Production*
Mary P. Ferguson

*www.maxwell.af.mil/au/aul/aupress*